THE ORCHID STORIES

Books by Kenward Elmslie

THE ORCHID STORIES

MOTOR DISTURBANCE

CIRCUS NERVES

ALBUM

THE CHAMP

THE ORCHID STORIES

KENWARD ELMSLIE

PARIS REVIEW EDITIONS

Doubleday & Company, Inc., 1973, Garden City, New York

Acknowledgement is made to the following publications in which these stories, subsequently revised, first appeared:

ADVENTURES IN POETRY: *"Waking Up"*; JUILLARD: *"My Holy City Geography Book," "Zoroaster"*; PARIS REVIEW: *"Accident Vertigo," "Locust Gleanings," "Moon Canal Morning," "Native Innards," "Eugene V. Debs' Last Mackintosh," "Hiatus: Orchid Ode," "Streetcar"*; REVISTA DE LETRAS: *"Fauteuil."*

ISBN: 0-385-07365-8
Library of Congress Catalog Card Number 70–157586

To
Maxine

CONTENTS

viii   CONTENTS

THE ORCHID STORIES

LOCUST GLEANINGS

Bubbers was standing on tiptoes, his wily face pressed against the bars of the entrance gate that led to a fine old Kentucky estate known as *Locust*. In her fifties—according to family legend—her—her—her—

Mattie and Bubbers talked of "low-cost" this and "low-cost" that—according to family legend—until Edith, tracing medieval castle patterns in the dust with her cane (turrets, walls, moat, outer walls, then funeral cortege of limousines, headlights on, in long line on Roman road), said, "Mattie, let's buy it and call it *Low Cost!*"
Bubbers—

The front façade was timbered in gently silvered pine. On the front door, an itinerant "two hands" painter had sketched three profiles (hands relaxed languorously against ear and cheek): Mattie and Edith and Bubbers. Every spring, an apprentice came around to touch up the colors, and, for several weeks, they looked heavily made up in a louche way, but, by mid-summer, the cheeks were ashen with small cracks proliferating here and there, and the lips were no longer Fire Engine Red, but Albino Eye Pink.

Eyes themselves? Dull and expressionless, like someone
pretending to be blind who can actually see.

The downstairs consisted of a sun porch filled with rub-
ber plants, wicker furniture, and ferns hanging in Indian
baskets from the Amazon, attached to gilt chains. Next:
the entrance hall, a circular room with three niches in one
wall in which three teakwood busts were set—Mattie and
Edith and Bubbers. The living room opened onto the
sequestered rose garden with the gap in the hedge through
which the ocean sparkled, the ocean actually being a huge
mural series painted on white marble slabs replete with
fishing smacks, liners, gulls, dolphins, a whale spout, and
several peopled life rafts. The dining room led to the
breakfast nook, pantry, kitchen, servants' kitchen, servants'
pantry, sleeping area, area for pets, out to the intercom
chamber and outside phone wall, down into the tunnels
through smelly dirt.

"Feel the cold pipes."

In her forties, Bubbers had—her—her—

Edith's nickname was Lady Knickers. That's what she
wore, for outings, according to family legend—afternoon
lie-downs, morning socials, the regattas, the golf matches,
the bridge competitions, the ghost story marathons on the
bluffs above the little city (zombie hands tighten on neck,
blobs of spectral wetness balloon out of mouth-and-nos-
trils)—and lazy rowboat expeditions down the forgotten
and disused canal system, where weeping willows drooped,
trailing small sere droppings that yellowed and hardened
into minute prickly balls every autumn . . .

Bubbers, in her thirties—her—her—

It had been autumn that time Mattie and she were
looking for a place to settle, and land around Hiramville

was dirt-cheap. An invasion of Acacians had displaced the
Scotch-Irish "Black-Spanish" mountaineers, rigorous Hu-
guenots who headed westward across the Wall of Lakes,
as they called it, fanning out into settlements on islands in
the N. P. Region, as they called it (New Paris? Netherlands
Papua?)—from where they wrote intensely codified letter-
poems of deaths and births to Mattie and Edith and Bub-
bers:

Matthew dear, Bet and Graciosa have finished their rabbit hutch.
Thanks to python miasma, they began to feel so out-of-touch

they undertook to build a covered bridge across the swamp.
Edith, they plan to take the mango harvest to P'touville where
    romp

mulatto brats in gutters, Bubbers, full of excrement and mushy
    fruit.
P'touville, sixty miles away, was built, Matthew, by some
    galoot

out of cartons, tins, driftwood, discarded ballast. Bug bites
turn one's skin into a fierce inferno. On summer nights

under protective nettings, we gather in front of Calvin's
    Shrine.
Surrounded by orchid bushes, his marble ruffle shimmers in
    the moonshine.

Baby Doda is dead, Edith. Terry breathed his last (ninety
    years old)
on Xmas Eve. Wet spring. The mangos are pre-sold,

and the Co-op, Bubbers, will gross eight million yen.
Angel statues now number (they intrigue the spider monkeys)
    ten.

Number Six is half-concealed by a bougainvillea bush,
a mere seedling last year. Matthew, its blossoms push

and sway against the orchid bushes around ⚹6's wings.
The contours of its face resemble yours, Edith. It sings,

Bubbers, somedays of Hiramville, canals, weeping willows in
     the snow,
or so it seems to those of us who miss you all. Love, Joe.

Edith whisked through European spas, till her penchant
for fronds came to a head. To The Islands! Batting at
leaves, drugged with heavy jungle odors, Edith, Mattie,
and Bubbers sat in their respective litters. Dressed formally,
"black-tie," they sat through excruciating meals.

Mattie died, of what nobody quite knew. Effluvia . . .
insects in it . . . blackens . . . found in portable tub . . .
all red . . . the water . . . return to settle estate: molasses
holdings, dabblings in "futures," railroad stocks, mines,
chrome wipers, crocks, iridescent hooks, Friendship Clubs,
barber shops, bull boxes, schools for training domestics, un-
guents, Orphan Associations, congestion research.

According to local legend, Bubbers met a young drifter:
Phil. They formed an immediate attachment, and soon, a
new profile was ensconced on the front door, replacing
Mattie's, and a plastic bust was set in Mattie's niche in the
entrance hall.

Scene: Deserted Fishing Camp.
Bubbers and Edith stare down through knot-hole gap
in floor-board. Phil is naked on cot, reading *Popular
Mechanics* he purchased in drugstore, along with comb,
pack of *Shadows*, pocketknife.

Three weeks later, Edith was found asphyxiated in a
motel bathroom, a bath mat soaked with chloroform over
her head, and, in one hand, a blue and pink mottled
"Locust" orchid, grown in the hot-house of Locust Man-
sion from a cutting sent by Joe. The hot-house was left
to Bubbers, everything else to Phil. In her twenties—her
—her—

Even in her teens, Edith enjoyed demise parodies, accord-
ing to family legend.

"Orchids take on the form of little birds, lizards, insects,
man, woman, of sinister fighters in a death embrace, of
lazy tortoises basking upside down in the sun, of agile and
ever chattering monkeys screened by fronds. If they don't
make us laugh, they surely excite—"

So saying, Edith likely as not'd rush from the room, slam
her door from behind which would issue forth the most
desperate noises (chokes, gasps, "HELP! MURDERER!
FIRE, FIRE!") and likely as not, a blood-colored liquid
(concocted via her chemistry set) would ooze out from
under the door as she'd go into her demise parody ("Send
for Father Pierre—it's my *coeur*"—"My life is whirling past:
hello, Mama Stephanie, hello Baby Doda, hello Genevieve's
baroque inner climate, someone smells of sourgrass, aha,
that old rancher Dade Morris, that's who, going backwards
now, people moving funnily, jumping up on diving-boards,
climbing off of trains backwards, hurrying up through the
sunset onto the cliff, climbing off of trains backwards,
they wave goodbye, then kiss their beloveds, and walk
backwards with their beloveds into a motor-car which
backs up into the distance, ha-ha, babies, goo-goo, babies,
climbing back into the black place, ha-ha, happy, ha-pp-
ee!!)—followed by a thump. Everyone'd rush inside, having
battered down the door only to see she'd fled out the win-

dow, having kicked chairs and tables in everyone's way, all along the verandah. Locked in the guest bathroom downstairs, she'd begin her Silent Treatment, except for a long succession of suspicious plop-plop sounds (stale bread carried in a bag tied around her neck, along with pebbles gathered on summer walks)—then, finally, a long sigh, "Ha-pp-ee!!!"—then the worst, a black foamy liquid dribbling out the door (referred to privately as "vampire excrement") and silence, irrevocable silence.

At this point, there was nothing left to do but creep away, and try to salvage the day; when she came down to dinner, no mention was made of Edith's demise parody penchant.

Bubbers handed me the "death" orchid, Edith's orchid, already brown.

"Throw it far, far away."

I went into the garden and walked to the cliff. I stared glumly at a peopled life raft. A tiny creature in a bespangled outfit was clinging to a chihuahua disconsolately. Girls in cage, mouths agape. Spray wet my kneecaps: lawn sprinkler. I put the orchid in my underwear, next to my sex.

Bubbers lay beside me, and cranked up his portable victrola to listen to *GILDA GREY*, his favorite moviestar operetta. The story of a silent screen star who falls on evil days, his favorite aria, *Alien Moon*, was sung by Gilda to a bellboy in her hotel room, in Alabama, overlooking the Gulf of Mexico.

GILDA:

> *Emergencies of the heart,*
> *Let me be.*
> *Alien moon.*
> *Gertrud has left,*
>   *The horror creature.*
>   *The sullen loungers*
>   *On the city dump*
>   *Picking through rusty entrails*
>   *(Bales and jails)*
>   *Are like sweet orchids of desire to me,*
>   *Descending on skeins of wire to me.*
>   *The luxury of neon at noon*
>   *Gives these skinny mountain boys*
>   *The pallor of an alien moon,*
>   *Alien moon.*
>   *Alien moon . . .*

I picked up the record and broke it on a red boulder. A deer stood watching me, from the edge of a forest across a huge ravine. The deer stomped, snorted, and continued to stare. I was filled with an overpowering awareness of birds and vines, of insects buzzing towards me, staring into my eyes, then continuing. This oneness went away, fast.

That night, we listened to the Death Scene of *GILDA GREY* on the Magnavox. A vinyl bust of me was set in Edith's niche in the entrance hall, and my profile was ensconced on the front door.

GILDA:

> *My life is whirling past,*
> > *Fire, fire!*
> > *Fire, fire!*
> *Wreckers' balls,*
> *Out of the tunnel they pour,*
> *Wreckers' balls,*
> *Pyramid above my pyre.*
>
> *Gilda cannot see the moon.*
> *Harvest, come soon.*
> > *Soon, harvest, soon.*

The machine went haywire at this point, spitting records all over the room, and into the ravine, outside the open loggia window. One sailed towards my bust and chipped off the nose, which teetered on the parquet, before coming to rest. Bubbers put on Edith's dark glasses. He told me to call him Mummers from then on, and I did.

NATIVE INNARDS

Mummers was wearing black and was in his early eighties. Spats, homburg, silk mourning bands around both sleeves and trouser legs (thigh-level)—black, all black. We had journeyed to a "white country," as he called it (Sweden), to take his mind off death.

Settling into the white sofa in our luxurious suite (all white appointments), he made a speech to us all:

MUMMERS:

> Stockholm's lifelessness is oppressive. Nothing is pockmarked, nothing is bloated or festering. No granules, no soft round squishy places in the asphalt make one feel protective towards The Venerable Albino—Stockholm. Protective because vulnerable. Because it isn't vulnerable. Summer should make the atmosphere quiver, city folk head for barns beyond the truck gardens, brown arms and legs, human bugs in the straw, down they fall to the amusement of the farmer and his wife and many little ones, a big supper, glad

*to share, dancers from Delaware, cadets from
California, thruway designers from Texas, Arctic
Circle, Arctic Circle, where was I? Summer
should make the atmosphere quiver, but here the
pathetic wisps of warmth lull leaves, branches,
and people into—into—into—an extremely in-
good-taste immobility redolent of the most
arrogant form of narcissism known to man:
Death. As that great astro-physicist, Sir William
Herschel, exclaimed when he saw a vast area of
sky that seemed to be totally starless:*

Heir ist wahrhaftig ein Loch in Himmel!
(Here is surely a hole in the sky!)

That afternoon, we took an express sea-bus to Oslo, and
changed to a fur trawler. We proceeded a considerable
distance north of Oslo, till we reached our destination:
White Island—cottage industries:

1. Ermine Processing.
2. Judge and Aristocrat Clothes.

On the way, we saw increasing numbers of ice chunks
drifting south, lime-and-violet in the dusk.

Mummers cheered up the following morning when he
encountered a retired opera singer who had once per-
formed in a production of *GILDA GREY* that toured
the Balkans for several years. All she could remember was
a fragment from the *Brown Derby Trio*.

GILDA:

Vrashti zooshf cvag Paramount e United Artists cvag
svashf bug cvag Pola e Sweet e Pickford
e Nita Naldi, Nita, Nita.
Monogram e bug cvag!
Republic e bug cvag!
Bug cvag!
Cvag!

For a modest fee, she agreed to take charge of us children. Her name was Gertrud.

By nightfall, Mummers was wearing white, even down to his spats and shoes.

That night, after Gertrud had hummed us to sleep, we crept to our verandah screen, and through the dank vines, watched Mummers and Mummy play auction bridge with a couple called the Schmidlapps.

Dr. Schmidlapp was a specialist in the upper respiratory tract. Every year, he came to White Island accompanied by his wife, Helga, and by a handful of devoted patients and followers. This particular summer, the following group had come to White Island with Dr. and Mrs. Schmidlapp:

GLADYS JACOMB . . . . *Cockney ex-vaudevillian*
DENNIS JACOMB . . . . *her husband, retired stevedore*
EVALYN B—— . . . . *hair designer*
GEORGIA B—— . . . . *chair shiner*
PATTI B———— . . . . *share combiner*
TERRI B———— . . . . *glare diviner*
ZITTI B———— . . . . *spare liner*
HERMAN OTT . . . . *automobile salesman*
GERTRUD . . . . *ex-opera singer (beer smell)*

Which one of these people grew the "Native Innards" orchid?

MRS. SCHMIDLAPP

I disliked Dr. Schmidlapp right off, as, for one thing, he tended to personalize nature. He was wont to refer to seeds as "expert hitchhikers," to say that sloths "tie on the old feedbag," and to liken the genes to a pack of cards, which is shuffled and arranged in many different ways, dealing each of us a "Grand Slam" or a "Full House." His second failing, I found, was his passion for dreams. Every morning, on the bulletin board by the lobby, he posted the dreams he'd dreamt the night before. Mrs. Schmidlapp did likewise, and, if the night had proved dreamless, they drew on some past dream that seemed pertinent. At breakfast, they'd circulate from table to table, through the dining room, notebooks in hand, jotting down the dreams of patients (orange juice, Herman Ott—cream of wheat, Gladys Jacomb—eggs sunnyside up, The B------ Sisters—coffee, us!) and non-patients alike.

According to Gertrud, who liked to chat about the Schmidlapps, Mrs. Schmidlapp had a great deal of free time, both in Florida, where they usually resided, and on White Island. Helga had little to do, in fact, as homemaker, for the doctor preferred to do the cooking when he came home from the lab, in order to "unwind," as he put it. Gertrud set me the chore of learning the menus of a typical week's dinners in Florida, to improve my memory. Happily for me, they ate simply:

MONDAY—

> *Easy Spaghetti   Cole Slaw*
> *Pronto Pups   Swiss Asparagus*
> *Grapenuts Puff Pudding*
> *Grape Cooler   Iced Coffee*
> *Bouncing Bunnies*

TUESDAY—

> *Jiffy Chicken   Cole Slaw*
> *Pronto Pups   Candied Carrots*
> *Cherry Surprise Balls*
> *Cherry Cooler   Iced Coffee*
> *Bouncing Bunnies*
> *Liqueur**

WEDNESDAY—

> *Seafood Okra Gumbo*
> *Prune Cake*
> *Prune Cooler*

THURSDAY—FRIDAY—SATURDAY
Repeats of the
MONDAY—TUESDAY—WEDNESDAY
Menus

SUNDAY—

> *Ham and Banana Batter Fried Sandwiches*
> *Pronto Pups   Swiss Asparagus*
> *Easy-Does-It Fruit Cake*
> *Maraschino Nut Fruit Clusters*
> *Maraschino Cooler   Iced Coffee*
> *Bouncing Bunnies*

---

* Average liqueur bottle would last them, say, five to seven weeks—when they'd run out, switch flavors, apricot cordial their favorite, then banana, then coffee.

Dr. Schmidlapp preferred to do the cooking, but she laid the table. Blue was Helga's favorite color, and so blue plates it was—"special" blue plates she called them. According to Gertrud, she had no close women friends, as the vapid chatter of the local doctors' wives got on her nerves. As far as men went, romantic dalliance was out of the question, as, according to Gertrud, she adhered to a rigid sexual schedule, which I had soon committed to memory.

MONDAY—

> Dr. S. is twelve-year-old boy in any big city, on recriminations. One personal belonging broken or destroyed in her bed. Changes into virgin when sharp fragments lacerate part of her body—thigh, ankle, scruff of neck. Dab her with iodine— purification ritual. He promises to repent, offers her a good home with guest cottages for her sisters: Evalyn, Georgia, Patti, Terri, and Zitti. Goes away to tell them the good news. She returns as Muriel, twin sister—a virgin. Changes into tart—police record, expulsion from country. Muriel initiates uprising, in forests, becomes dictator. She falls asleep in pasture. Dr. S. returns (sailor)—watches her happily. Wakes up. Happy reunion. Retire to cattle ranch in interior.

TUESDAY—

> Dr. S. is twelve-year-old boy in any big city, on his Easter vacation. Sexual favorite of sadistic headmaster in prep school on the moors: flogging and buggery. She's bosomy waitress in Black Magic Tea Room, dominated by mannish

*fortune-teller in back room—Giselle. Waitress takes
boy home at dusk—acne poultice. Dingy shack.
He can't get aroused. In icebox, orchid Giselle
has given her: amulet power. They eat it in
batter fried sandwich, as joke. She puts acne
poultice on him, leaps up, forces her to floor.
Inexhaustible sex prowess. Same with her. Each
keeps eyes shut, visualizes other as "Giselle." He
moves in with her, leaves prep school, works as
dish-washer. Very happy together. Knock at door,
Friday the 13th. Voice: Giselle's.*

WEDNESDAY—

*Helga is twelve-year-old native beauty in South
America. He is German tourist, pre-World War I.
Jungle episode: attack of toucans. Leaf-cutter ants.
Blackwater fever, drift downstream on log, sex
hallucinations involving animals: crocodile,
rhino. Hiram the Frog. An outpost. Teaches her
rudiments of German. Pregnancy. Radio report
of Armistice Day. Leaves her—exchange orchid,
torn in half. Dugout canoe. Sex. Farewell, toot of
steamer.*

THURSDAY—FRIDAY—SATURDAY
Repeats of the
MONDAY—TUESDAY—WEDNESDAY
Sex Schedule

SUNDAY—

*They bathe together, fellow patients in an asylum
for the well-to-do. Immediate attraction, etc.
Escape in laundry truck to any big city. Jobs,*

nice apartment, money, success. Grow orchids in
penthouse greenhouse. "Native Innards" orchid
always in bloom. Trace designs on each other
with it. Foreplay. Write words. More foreplay. Go
to sleep, intertwined.

To fill her empty Florida days, Helga invented a port-
able greenhouse. The window-pane sections moved on
slats in such a way that they folded, accordion-style, fit-
ting into four largish padded boxes. Dr. Schmidlapp could
assemble the greenhouse easily in an afternoon, assisted
by the "traveling" patients. Mrs. Schmidlapp's greenhouse
sat directly outside our room, on the far edge of the spa-
cious hotel lawn. By now, the hotel guests accepted the
glass-and-chrome structure as evidence of summer, along
with the holly tree blossoms, the avid insects, and the lazy
hummy sounds of any hot day anywhere. She always
traveled to Norway with the greenhouse, for the doctor's
vacation routine was not so dissimilar to his workaday
routine. Both revolved around constant scientific research
to lessen (goal: eliminate) his patients' breath problems.
He spared no one, least of all himself, and often his
world was confined to batches of bottles with labels which
had to be kept at a constant temperature and shaken up at
specific intervals; readings had to be jotted down and
collated. In the bottles were phlegm samples, scrapings
from lungs, throat matter, saliva, gum samples, scrapings
from teeth, scrapings from throat skin, gorge skin, mouth
skin, gum skin, face skin, tongue skin, gland skin, plus
food decay pieces (two hours after eating, four hours
after etc.)—all taken at specific intervals.

Dr. Schmidlapp was obsessed, according to Gertrud, by

the inter-relationships between air, weather, family ties, dreams, and "breath pulse."

Several years in the past, one of his grateful patients had sent Mrs. Schmidlapp a cutting from a relative's coffee finca in the interior of Colombia. This cutting had flowered (according to Gertrud) the day before our arrival, sending both Dr. and Mrs. Schmidlapp into transports of delight. It was definitely a "Native Innards": their first! It had a purplish velvety surface, and an inner opening that was black streaked with green, like the markings of a wasp, surrounded by a pumpkin-orange band, bumpy and sticky at night, smooth and concave by day. Gertrud chattered so incessantly about this mere flower, with such evident longing, Mummers and Mummy hit on a plan.

Mummy went into Oslo the next day and bought a night watchman's outfit, overalls and flashlight and all, plus a sheepwool coat, hooded with a string system to close the face opening to a size commensurate with the weather. Mummy put it on as soon as she returned to White Island, and lay down on her bed, too exhausted to go down to dinner. We left her, and sat down at our usual table, next to Dr. and Mrs. Schmidlapp. According to the bulletin board, tonight was the night they intended to snip the "Native Innards" blossom, and take it to their quarters. The "P.S." requested "DO NOT DISTURB US FOR 48 HOURS, THANKS."

They were eating heartily of the regular Friday fare:

Melon and Westphalian Ham
Marrow on Toast
Fondue—the Swiss National Dish—

(little pieces of filet mignon
individually dipped into sizzling
peanut oil). Lots of sauces which
each guest dipped meat chunks
in after they were sufficiently
cooked in the peanut oil
which simmered at each table in
receptacles kept warm by Bunsen
burners. For dessert, the guests had their choice of—

I rushed upstairs to warn Mummy. The plan was for
Mummy, in her night watchman disguise, to creep into
the greenhouse while the Schmidlapps were eating, and
snip off the orchid, hiding it under her sheepwool coat.
Mummers was to be look-out, and us children were to
keep the Schmidlapps occupied by telling them a slew
of afternoon nap hot dreams—flying through clouds at
sunrise, solo, dipping down close to tree-tops, skimming
up—crone in tree outside bedroom window paralyzes us
kids—hoopy tunnel, plummet down it—then Mummy'd
slip the orchid under Gertrud's pillow: mystery gift!

Mummy was standing upright on the bed, in her night
watchman disguise, and her pants were around her knees.
Mummers was kneeling in front of her. Blurry here—
impenetrable memory gap—nausea—"woozy baby"—whis-
pers, "Phil . . . Phil . . . oh Phil . . ."—big red—I shut
the door fast, and by the time Mummy was ready, the
Schmidlapps had finished their demitasses, and had strolled
over to the greenhouse. Fortunately, it being Midsummer
Eve, they'd decided to snip it at midnight, when the sun
was scheduled to finally sink.

The upshot of the matter was: Mummers slipped out
at eleven that night, while everyone was carousing around

the pool, and snipped off "Native Innards" with Mummy's nail scissors. He rushed back upstairs, and tiptoed into Gertrud's room (us children were keeping Gertrud busy at the pool) and slipped the orchid under her pillow, according to plan. Unfortunately, Dr. Schmidlapp was asleep on the corridor sofa with Mrs. Schmidlapp, directly opposite Gertrud's room. In his haste, Mummers slammed Gertrud's bedroom door, while leaving. Dr. Schmidlapp awakened with a start from a dream of a gun fired by a bandit, again and again, first at his patients, then his wife, then—as the gun was aimed in his direction, he woke up. He sat bolt upright, and in so doing, yanked a lap-robe off his wife. The crisp night air made her shiver, and she (all this was on the bulletin board the following A.M.) dreamed of a labyrinth in an iceberg, comprised of chilly chasms and caverns. Unable to move her legs, which were asleep, she noticed Eskimo troops silhouetted on the edge of the volcano-shaped rim at the center of which she lay. Her mouth was sealed with bandage tapes ("X" pattern) and she couldn't breathe. To her left, a crowd was attempting to inch through a small egress in the snow, a simple hole that looked as if it had been dug by some arctic creature in search of a hibernation cubbyhole. Angrily, the crowd turned on her, as if their slow progress were somehow her fault, and at this point, she woke up, a few scant seconds after her husband. Not surprisingly, they couldn't sleep another wink that night. Midnight rolled around. Dr. Schmidlapp discovered the theft! Helga became hysterical, and marched into Gertrud's room, followed by Gertrud, who became hysterical, protesting her innocence. At which point, I lifted the pillow. Helga screamed! Dr. Schmidlapp paled, and Gertrud began weeping. She hurled the orchid at me, and I ran from the room. We could hear sobs and screams till the sun rose at 3 A.M. The sickly yellow dawn quieted everyone down.

We left the next day, with the "Native Innards" tucked in George (my younger half-brother's) birdcage, packed into an empty Lucky Strike carton, on a cushion of moss, concealed by a tattered tarpaulin cover. Helga could be seen, lying on the earth floor of the greenhouse, immobile. Dr. Schmidlapp had moved Gertrud's skimpy possessions into his beach mansion.

We didn't say goodbye, though Mummers did slip a gratuity under the kitchen door of the beach mansion, inscribed "For Gertrud." Mummy left her night watchman outfit behind, and I sometimes wonder what the manager must have thought when he opened the closet door and saw her regalia.

On the fur trawler to Oslo, I made a list of words on a black-bordered piece of grief stationery. I got up to eleven:

> *Philadelphia*
> *fill*
> *philander*
> *fillip*
> *philtre*
> *filter*
> *filigree*
> *philodendron*
> *philosophy*
> *philology*
> *philippic*

I showed Mummy my list. Mummy added one word to my list, saying,

"Cheaper by the dozen!"

I lay down in her lap, complaining of seasickness, though I felt fine. Mummy scratched my head all the way to

Oslo, and incredible tingles coursed through me. Total happiness. On the pier, I unfolded the grief stationery, though I knew what the added word would be:

Phil

We took a luxury liner to New York. A party of us went to the graveyard where Edith and Mattie lay buried, in the garden at Locust, behind the peopled life raft with the tiny creature in the bespangled outfit clinging to it. With Mummy's consent, I placed "Native Innards" on the soil, where a few blades of grass were beginning to lengthen and droop—wilted by the summer drought. We passed the orchid from hand to hand; actually, Mummy helped me place the orchid on the soil. She took off her black veil, her black blouse, and her black slacks, and slipped into a white summer dress. Mummers was in white, as usual, but he had to hold up the blanket while Mummy changed. Mummy (a year after Mummers brought her home, he asked us to call her that, and we did) bent down, retrieved the orchid, put it back in its Lucky Strike carton, and we clambered into the spacious limousine hired for the occasion.

When we reached Hode, it was my duty to put the orchid (my orchid, Mummy insisted, scratching my hair just the way I liked) in the attic, under an eye-shaped window. All I remember (up there) was the unbearable heat, and motes in the air, and my fear of fainting (Mummers was on the stairs, peering at me), and the feeling of time suspended: infinite days.

EUGENE V. DEBS' LAST MACKINTOSH

I

The skin of my face has a certain amount of color of its own, but the main part of the color of my face is the blood shining thru my skin. It is my heart that drives the blood thru the skin of my face. When a person is frightened, the nerve running from his brain to his heart interferes so with his circulation, scarcely any blood is sent thru the blood vessels, directly underneath the skin of the face. We see pallor, the color of true memory—white.

—EUGENE V. DEBS

White is the color of true memory, I soon discerned. The pale green of old fjords changes to a vivid emerald hue in retrospect, and the foam of old oceans grows more and more violent, till rainbows in the spume bubbles start arching this way and that. Each spectrum starts drawing attention to itself—until what might have been a true memory veers into the realm of hallucination. In my bed, before singing myself to sleep with old arias (". . . *neon at noon* . . ."), I'd think of the faded and peeling pink of the attic planks upstairs, and me, squatting, drinking a cherry phosphate at sunset—and the memory would veer away into Fire Engine Red. Something had to be done to eliminate these shifts.

Ah, for the simplicity of white clouds, white rain, mists enveloping clean white cities. Crazy white boulevards slanting up and up into silver fogs, fogs that hide people's heads and ankles in one lane, and in an adjacent lane, only middle sections are visible: pregnant women and men with huge bellies, laughing and holding hands.

Ah, for the calm of sidewalks. Mica! First pavement stone. Crack. Second pavement stone. Crack. Distancing! The tiny camera (oneself) jounces along, films the crack-and-pavement alternation, bumping along at a fast clip. Chip away at the pavement, until the crack forms a curve —grooves form along the edge of the curve, and a whole grooved circle starts revolving as one hovers over it, filming away. And out of it, messages galore pour forth, relayed from open windows, grates, feeder-megaphones, machinery left in the gulches—

> *"This is Eugene V. Debs, your childhood hero.*
> *How white my cell is. And how white the votes*
> *in the presidential election. They have just sent*
> *me a sample ballot disqualified as fraudulent.*
> *Stapled over the 'X' in the box beside my name,*
> *under Coolidge, Wilson, La Follette, and above*
> *the splinter parties—dream vigor puff—growing*
> *incoherent, lad, it's the poultice on my forehead,*
> *the chloroform, certain forces out to—stapled*
> *over the 'X' in the box beside my name, are*
> *graffiti of an asparagus poised above an ear, with*

a diamond earring shaped like a harvest moon,
with a tiny man carrying a sickle (made of seed-
pearls) and towards the ear, drops of something
plummet, ten in number. Five is named
EUGENE V. DEBS' LAST MACKINTOSH.
Ssshhh. Ssshhh."

White clouds, white rain, white mists swirling. Ssshhh!
Ssshhh! Life is whirling past. Vision of Mayan Indian.
Squat brown body. Lives by roadside, pretends to be asleep.
I sense he is watching my progress through the whiteness
that turns into a noisy jungle. Scooping people up from
one place to another isn't hard for him, as he knows how
to climb into the crack between the whiteness of true
memory and the whiteness of winter weather as seen
through an eye-shaped attic window, cherry phosphate
in one hand, and on the battered turntable, a worn-out
record that keeps repeating one word, "Whoa!"—which
turns into a second message:

"There are three main reasons for the loss of
ancient history. We know we find black folks
living in the hottest parts of the earth, in many
places where white men find it uncomfortable to
live. So they try to make a boodle, and head
back to pleasure zones, where the mornings are
cool, and the butterflies small, and at night, all is
quiet except for a cricket—or a train whistle.
They take off their clothes and pass the night,
making love. They wipe each other off, and it
is Love Sweat they wipe off, not Heat Sweat.
Evidently, black folks serve as shields that fend
off the abyss of climate horror, guarding the
frontiers, so that ancient history can be

conveniently collected and gathered into learning centers. However, these frontiers are our future horizons. Us whites, I mean. Second, the higher up we are, we can look around the sides of an object a little, and this helps us see how solid the object is, how deep in front or behind. But, third, in our aerial shield, on the frontier, we are in trouble . . . things more and more blanch, until a craven need for man-made jungles obsesses the city-dweller. You see, the loss of ancient history has been so total, the networks of plastic shrubbery that reflect the seasons (turn green, droop, glitter) obscure familiar routes (grocery store to pawnshop to bakery to beauty parlor vs. barbershop to pool hall to cigar store to public baths to park bench). Connections break down, except via circuitous underground paths, chiseled painstakingly through solid rock, by the conquered. I see no possible solution, and that's why I ran for office—so people would realize the gravity of the situation. I sit here in my cell, awaiting my purgatory:

A) TRIP TO JUNGLE

B) SEARCH FOR FLOWER

C) ASCENT TO HEAVEN

Winter in Atlanta is cold. Stone universe. The Jungle is the proletariat, awaiting the white hurricane of social justice that will restore the basic social unit of the tribal encampment, thereby putting mankind back in touch with ancient history. The flower is—foo, Eugene. Don't defoliate your interior. Simply move on, and on some more! And whoever finds this circle of

sound, look in my mackintosh, the mackintosh
the prison guards impounded upon my admission,
and in the right pocket—foo! The guard!
Message ess . . ."

Tree frogs chatter. Violent perfumes. In swift succession, sandalwood gives way to a dead fish stink, which gives way to a synthetic face-powder smell. The Mayan in his pseudo-sleep holds up two placards:

AN ASPARAGUS
AN EAR

He places the asparagus behind the ear, and miraculously, a flower forms—to my great joy, an orchid: all-white. The Mayan vanishes, and the orchid diminishes in size, grotesquely, as if it were being deflated while being carried along a tunnel with brilliant light coming through its far end. Dropping sensation. Trapdoor in aeroplane has sprung open, releasing me into pure sky. Fall through whiteness. Flower reappears directly below me. I fall into it. Round chamber. Antennae brush my entire body, which is naked. I notice, with a heavy feeling of dread, that the chamber isn't really round. It's ear-shaped. My penis stiffens, and, though I feel no excitation, ten drops of semen issue from it, and float in the air, circling around me weightlessly. One by one, they enter my ear, blocking all but the following nine words, the third message:

Man.
Intelligent.
Beings.
Enemies.
Africa.
Act for.
Or show.

II

It was in August I discovered the "Debs" white orchid, across the river from Hode, in its twin city, Spode. Specifically, it was in the Clothing Wing of the Wealth Museum. Mummers and I were standing in front of ferns painted white, with sleeping Mayan faces sort of floating among them—three-dimensional—decorating the three sides of an exhibit, a replica of a prison cell. A naked lightbulb hung from the ceiling, swaying slightly, as if someone had just jostled it. A gaunt mannequin with sagging shoulders and a creased forehead lay on the middle tier of a triple-tiered bunk. He was lying with a mackintosh draped over him, like a blanket. Identical mackintoshes lay on the top and bottom tiers. I noticed a label, in the exhibit itself, pasted to the right of the bunk, crudely lettered in pencil and signed by "Mother Bloor":

EUGENE V. DEBS' LAST MACKINTOSH

ATLANTA PEN   1923

As I peered at the exhibit, a quotation from Ralph Waldo Emerson came to mind:

"Every hero becomes a bore at last."

III

I waited until the guard had passed down the corridor,
past the CAGE OF EAGLES (Lindbergh in goggles—sea gulls
—cumulus cloud—French voices on radio—swats at fly on
instrument panel—Hitler and Mussolini in mid-air with
wings attached trying to keep up, panting and red-faced)
and EASTER ON THE FIRST SUBMARINE (air malfunctioning
—red alert—gong—the men are drinking whiskey—suck
air from each other's lungs—chaplain has pipes coming
out of chest, officers suck on pipes—enlisted men sit around
waiting their turn). I crept under the glass panel, and
crawled across the floor and under the bottom bunk. Mum-
mers looked wide-eyed with horror, and his fists beat
against the glass, silently. I cut a hole in the bottom
mattress with my jackknife. I looked into the tunnel-like
hole, and, by lighting a match, I could see the contours
of a mackintosh pocket above me. I removed it, and
painstakingly got it through the mattress hole. To my
astonishment, in it was one third of a white orchid, made
out of some synthetic material, pliable and glossy. On one

petal was scrawled, with an effect as offensive as that of an obscene tattoo of sexual congress on a child's private parts:

A) TRIP TO JUNGLE

The guard returned. Mummers bent down and tied his shoelace, thereby blocking, by his girth, the guard's view of the area under the bottom bunk, where I lay curled up, holding my breath. I heard him clomp down the hall, and in the distance, a water fountain gurgled and stopped. I climbed up into the bottom bunk, and, huddling under the mackintosh, I again took out my knife. Cut. Tunnel hole. Look through. Mackintosh pocket. Reach in. Feel object. Retrieve. Second third of white orchid! Scrawled on it:

B) SEARCH FOR FLOWER

Climb up into middle bunk, spoon position against mannequin. Face to face—wedged between it and wall somehow. Words of final message—hear part of it, then silence, part of it, silence—

1. Is the Most—
2. Of living—
3. To escape his—
4. He spread into Europe and—
5. He cannot—
6. Himself—
7. What he likes—

Guard returns. Mummers offers him cigarette—against regulations. Edges him around so back faces exhibit. Bicker. Knife . . . cut . . . tunnel . . . pocket . . . object . . . retrieve . . . scrawl:

C) ASCENT TO HEAVEN

The guard walked away. The orchid was now complete. At that moment, I looked up. The lightbulb blinded me, and it seemed to be swinging in increasing arcs. On it was written circularly:

I

X   C

O   E

B

Something about the swinging aroused me sexually, and, next thing I knew, the nine words of Debs' third message came to me . . . and it seemed obvious . . . blocked by the ten drops entering my ear . . . drops of semen . . . the mystery words I'd just heard . . .

Quickly, I put together the message Debs must have considered so essential:

> *Man is the most intelligent*
> *of living beings. To escape*
> *his enemies, he spread into*
> *Europe and Africa. He cannot*
> *act for himself or show what*
> *he likes.*

I looked back up at the lightbulb, which had now quieted down. The frosted outline of the white orchid, with its three divisions, and its tripartite "journey," could be seen, surrounding the "ICEBOX." Ignoring the pain, I unscrewed it, then—orchid in pocket, I squeezed out of the exhibit. I handed the lightbulb to Mummers, but I put the synthetic orchid in the "Native Innards" box. The message I kept secret.

STREETCAR

On a streetcar in Hode, Arkansas, an odd incident happened. I was on my way downtown to the movies, a real Saturday excursion: banana fritters at the bus terminal café, then candy bombs from Frude's (I referred to bonbons as *bombs* at that age) which I would count, and as each cinnamon and lemon and cardamon pellet was tiny, I brought envelopes and always allotted at least thirty minutes for this—now I mention it, my counting mania was so powerful, little except counting during the day happened. Telephone poles. Cracks in the sidewalk. Power transmission substations, straddling fields like chrome giants. From Mount Ozark, I once counted eighty-two—tracing them along a valley that changed to a red-dust prairie at the state line.

My counting mania included my own skinny body. How long I could hold my breath. How long I could pee. Or how many times I could rub my member against my leg up and down without a blue nation occurring, "blue nation" being my term for ejaculation, which I thought meant "swear-word." I don't recall how I arrived at "blue nation," except that I always thought of oceans as nations in my dog-eared Rand McNally; in fact they seemed the biggest nations in the world as far as land areas were concerned, and I evolved whole honey-combed fantasies of the King of the Blue Nation of the Pacific Ocean, blue of course because they were blue in the atlas—the water areas.

This particular day, I got on a streetcar in Hode, Arkansas, on my way downtown to the movies, a real Saturday adventure. I had just locked myself in the guest bathroom downstairs with the nice little pink towels and perfumed soap with the gooey underside (Geraldine, the cook, secretly used to use it to get rid of the fish and garlic odor on her hands which she claimed kitchen soap —"Ivory" —didn't do) and had taken down my pants to stare, bent down, between my legs at my rear-end in the full-length mirror. I counted six "acid underwear transom wallops." Far from atypical in any lad's development, that's what Mummers called the blotches on my behind: "acid underwear transom wallops." He often made up word meanings. "Alligator" was his word for "elevator." On our first trip to Rose Park, we went to the observation booth at the top of the sandstone natural formation nicknamed "The Kiss Guns." At night, searchlight beams picked out the phosphorescent sails of the rafts of the wetbacks on their way to new harvests far below. We waited in front of the closed door with numbers that flickered on and off above its top edge. Two round black buttons at breast level had UP and DOWN printed in red. Mummers pushed UP. He mumbled about smelly excursionists confined in an airless space, and how he dreaded "closets that bump." The numbers blinked 6, then 5, then 4. Mummers shouted, "Where can that silly snip of an alligator-girl be?"

I ran out onto the mesa to escape this dreadful monster with ordinary legs, wearing a skirt no doubt, with an ordinary torso and arms, perhaps accoutered in a frilly blouse, but with gaping jaws and glittering rows of pointed teeth ready and waiting to chomp me to bits and pieces. I clutched the cold rocks, and sobbed and sobbed. Then I went back, and you can bet I went up by foot, around and around the cagelike stairway. The view was a distinct disappointment. It was twilight, when the sun on the horizon seems to flatten into an orange pie-dish surrounded by mauve bushes heavy with wispy white "semen-in-the-bathtub" excrescences. A lunar moth battered against the glass, leaving pea-green flecks behind. Time to go! Phil was impatient to get back to Locust Enterprises, Kentucky. Back down the cage! As luck would have it, just as I reached the ground floor, I let out a yelp. The "alligator" door opened to disgorge Mummers, Phil, Puppy Mack, and Jo-Anne! Instead of the monster creature I dreaded, I saw a pretty girl in a Civil War-type hoop skirt with a calico sunbonnet and long white gloves on.

"Observation booth," she trilled.

Everyone had a good laugh at my bewildered expression.

Might as well mention always had great trouble pinning down what "allegation" means. Always conjures up pictures of hills, scalloped Swiss Alps, with neat ski furrows, sky rides, luminous clouds of midges, the gabled roofs of Danzig near the waterfront with those festoons of gray chains that so fascinated Rilke, Genet, Borges, and Gogol.

Vehicles have always made me nervous, and the Maple Street streetcar of Hode, Arkansas, was no exception. When I woke up that morning, I was resolved to go on a Saturday excursion. I decided to see *Dog Roots* at the

Health Museum, for the third time. It was an absolutely pure kinetic map of elongated greenish and white blobs that adhered tenaciously to a barren earth surface (yes— definitely mesa-like) until dome-shaped cell growths began to proliferate at an accelerating tempo, first sluggishly uncoiling and breathing slowly, with long pauses for tiny involuntary quiverings, during which times fungus growths seeped out of gill-like apertures. Yellow and green, they sparkled like the snowiest landscape anyone could imagine, only to disappear back into the cell growths as the breathing process quickened. The point, so-called, and at that age everything still had a point as far as I was concerned, was this: the fungus growths and dome-shaped cells were totally interdependent—one could not survive without the other. For, as the final section of *Dog Roots* made clear, the cells, being deficient in storage tissue and growth-promoting factors, were incapable of attaining improved growth rates. Comparing the shape and differentiation of the cells, the film showed how the synthesis of niacin played an important part in the organism's pathway through life similar if not identical to the—

The film broke off here, as the information was not complete. Music was played, a national anthems medley, and the lights in the auditorium came on. After a pause, the movie resumed: images of mammals and certain bread molds equally susceptible to synthesis of niacin. The movie concluded that fungus had an absolutely essential role in supplying vitamins and sustenance to the dome-shaped cells. The mechanism of differentiation, the role of the genetic code, the unusual relationship between the code and differentiation, hinged on the anatomical and chemical changes wrought by fungus, providing the film's denouement: cells formed a female breast out of which spurted a dark cloud (our old friend—fungus) which was dissipated

into air, then rain, then snow, which fell on a New Eng-
landish town replete with white picket fences and white
church tower, houses, barns, etc. People appeared on their
way to church dressed in white, as Pilgrim Fathers, fol-
lowed at a distance by a knot of Pilgrim Mothers, camou-
flaged in weathered red: mobile barn. And in their midst,
unseen, the children. A hymn—"Jesus The Beautiful"—
came out of a loudspeaker in the bandstand at the center of
the plaza. A man in a black sombrero passed, carrying a
shovel. Nightfall. Digging scene. In the soil, the movement
of cells proliferating was caught, recapitulating the growth
and breath process—gills, fungus clouds, the formation of
deadly black blossoms. The blossoms blurred as they in-
creased in number, covering the round hillock. The cam-
era, weaving up to the horizon with a droopy-drawers
motion, introduced a new vantage point, which turned
the hillock into an unmistakable human breast out of
which issued fungus. Symbiosis!

Whole days passed when I rarely left my room. Fri-
day night, I could barely sleep so involved was I in my
Saturday excursion to see *Dog Roots*. I rehearsed getting
on the streetcar in my mind's eye—the steps, reaching
in my coat pocket for the three pennies, saying hi to the
uniformed traffic watcher. In point of fact, a new traffic
watcher was sitting in the green booth beside the cur-
tained conductor. A bunch of loud women got on, wear-
ing minks and orchids. A bony girl in her teens with
steel-rimmed spectacles and braces on her teeth accom-
panied them. In one hand, she held a pink noisemaker, and
on the lapel of her white velvet break-away coat, a blue-
and-gray orchid was pinned. I stared at it so relentlessly,
she tossed it to me, with studied nonchalance. Her party
got off at the next stop, opposite the Health Museum. I

had decided to get off several stops further on, and then walk back to the Health Museum, influenced by a momentary obsession that the curtained conductor might see me heading for the Museum and might surmise I was seeing *Dog Roots* for the third time—it seemed all too probable he'd remember the preceding Saturdays I'd gotten off at this same stop, at around the same time in order to catch the early morning show. I pried the streetcar window open and threw the orchid at her feet, shouting, "What's your name?"

At that moment, the traffic light changed from red to yellow, and she was forced to hurry across the street, urged on by the loud mink women. Green. An open convertible with a young couple in it obliterated the orchid. I kept thinking with fury how the petals would stick to the elephant trunk-colored tires. At that moment, the light changed to red, just as three armament trucks pulled up, jammed with soldiers surrounding a hooded weapon that was carried in the first vehicle, with an extension that was tied to the second and third vehicles. A group of factory workers crowded onto the streetcar, burly men from some Balkan culture, judging from their heavy mustaches and swart complexions. The ticket-taker, evidently an inexperienced replacement, was having difficulty making change. She had handed one of the factory workers a Mexican peso he refused to accept, affronted by what he took to be a racial slur of sorts. In addition, four members of a holy order were loath to get off the streetcar in full view of the soldiers in the armament trucks. The ticket-taker was remonstrating with the conductor (through the curtain, which she kept poking, as if hunting for the conductor) not to start up the streetcar until the monks could step onto the traffic island with impunity. As it was, the soldiers saw the monks standing by the open exit, and

ing in an exaggeratedly effeminate manner, the soldiers
pantomimed putting lipstick on, smoothing down their
eyebrows, forming spitcurls, while others more daring
pulled up imaginary skirts salaciously, wiggling their bod-
ies like monstrous showgirls, while still others imitated
attitudes of reverence and devotion. Pointing to their
hands with amazement, two soldiers, apparently identical
twins, rejoiced at the discovery of stigmata. The light
changed again, and the situation resolved itself—the three
armament trucks with a grinding of gears moved off,
prompting the soldiers to enact a ballet of gaucherie.
Thrown off balance by the motion of the trucks, they
clung to each other, as if for dear life, giggling and primp-
ing like silly schoolgirls. One of the monks snapped his
fingers as if he'd forgotten something important, tapping
his head with his forefinger three times to show how addled
he was. He sat back down, and the others did likewise.
Their decision to remain on the streetcar prompted a new
interchange between the conductor and the ticket-taker.
The factory workers, inflamed by their comrade's hurt,
were bearing down on the ticket-taker and conductor. The
cars at the intersection had by this time moved past, and the
traffic watcher pressed the go ahead buzzer. I could see the
entrance to the Health Museum. The mink ladies were
lined up in front of a revolving door, watching the girl
revolve and revolve.

MOONING

I felt something bosomy pressing against me. I opened my eyes, and craned around. It was Mummers. His lips were moving rapidly. He squatted down beside me. I took the wads of cotton out of my ears.

". . . to share whatever it is you're experiencing . . . not a stickler for everyday reality so-called . . . ha! . . . see by your eyes you're onto something . . . layers . . . not forcing . . . trust . . . mutual trust . . . wouldn't force anything . . . privacy . . . particulars . . . not forcing you."

I said no.

A diatribe followed, difficult for me to make much sense of—an attack on everyday reality, "Satanic" trick, any logical system that can be laid out can be controlled by viewer, dangerous, imposed on other viewers who become feeder stations to original viewer, vision widened with auxiliary antennae—distance between center and perimeter so immense, visions become garbled—weird statistics become law—misplaced zeros—cow is elected President of Meat Board (regulation to implement

democratic process)—enforced Daily Poet Celebrations
(regulation to implement anarchy necessary to weeding out
of outworn regulations)—newsflash: Venice has sunk—all
cities try to figure out how to sink (regulation to—to—
layers—fragments—)

Mummers gave up.

". . . all this mooning in the attic!"

I put the wads of cotton in my ears. When I looked
sideways, he'd gone.

What Mummers referred to derisively as "mooning-in-
the-attic" was actually a highly demanding but deeply
exhilarating ritual I'd evolved, after much trial and error,
thanks to a pamphlet I discovered by chance. The cir-
cumstances were these: after glimpsing the girl revolv-
ing and revolving at the Health Museum, I was trans-
ported into a state of such total ecstasy, I was afraid to
get off the streetcar at the next stop, as I'd planned, out
of terror that any sudden motion would shatter this ec-
stasy, disintegrating it into tedious fragments, bickering
little humdrum fragments that would grow tinier, pettier,
and more numerous with each step I took towards the
Health Museum, the very source of my ecstasy. Generally,
I didn't feel too involved in what was going on around
me, and while I enjoyed being a spectator (one never
knew what one would see)—this ecstasy state was infi-
nitely preferable to my customary spectator state. What
to do? A second problem: a second sight of the *Dog Roots*
girl might blur the clarity of the first sight of her revolv-
ing and revolving, a clarity that had triggered the ecstasy, a
clarity more beautiful than anything I'd ever seen. A third
problem: the longer I remained on the streetcar, the surer I
became that the ecstasy the sight of her revolving and re-
volving had released in me was so intense, it could

heighten the intensity of "everyday reality" around me, transforming it into a heightened state where anything could happen, that is—anything I willed. I was convinced a magic power was within my grasp, and, if only I wished it, the streetcar would grind to a stop, to the conductor's amazement, inexorably reverse directions, and, obeying the dictates of my desire, zoom past stops, clang through intersections, hurtling backwards till it arrived back at the Health Museum in time for me to see my vision again, still revolving and revolving.

Actually, the streetcar continued on its circular route—past the museum district, past the Chair Museum, the Museum of Happiness, the Museum of Fraternal Organizations, the Beauty Parlor Museum, and the Wealth Museum—then past the shopping district, down to the river, along the river to the amusement area, past its flashing lights and silhouetted rides to the factory gulch, which concealed the false city of tin shacks and mud huts, and —back to the residential area in the heights where I'd originally gotten on.

By now, I was in a state of total dejection at having lost my ecstasy source (the revolving girl) forever, as well as having missed *Dog Roots*. Next week, *Fog Toots* would be playing, a horror film about night-flying lepers who arouse Air Force pilots with their strong foxy odor.

The streetcar slowed down: time to get off. I felt like a zombie oldster whose sole remaining interest in life is to find a warm body of water to ease into—permanently. I happened to notice a pamphlet on the floor, dropped by one of the mink ladies. I picked it up (perhaps "she" had touched it) and got off the streetcar, wondering if I'd found a rescuer.

A rescuer it was. By studying the pamphlet (*The Yankee Way of Knowledge*) assiduously, I hit on a means of perpetuating the clarity of my "Dog Roots Girl" memory —my only source of ecstasy. As a bonus, I also stood a good chance of becoming A Man of Knowledge by conquering Four Life Obstacles:

1. FEAR
2. CLARITY
3. POWER
4. OLD AGE

This was the life goal the pamphlet dealt with, and this is how I adapted its tenets to my own individual ritual:

1. CONQUER FIRST LIFE OBSTACLE—

FEAR

Stare at "Native Innards" box, into which I'd sneaked dried remnants of "Edith's Death" orchid. Try not to blink. Hold breath. When box starts to glow and pulsate with shimmering light, resume blinking and breathing. Move about attic like protozoic blob, until comfortable Chain of Being spot on floor is found, spot that feels like right position in Evolution Cosmos. Lie down. Resume staring at "Native Innards" box, into which I'd sneaked dried, squashed remnants of "Dog Roots Girl" orchid, retrieved day after ecstasy incident—petals caught in asphalt squishy place near traffic island—scraped them off. Try not to blink. Hold breath. When box starts to shimmer with favorite color (crimson in my case, color of blood coming out of gash on one's arm on sparkly blue day)—resume blinking and breathe deeply. Breathe deeply. Keep it up.

*Breathe deeply, deeply. Breathe deeply. Breathe
deeply.*

2. CONQUER SECOND LIFE OBSTACLE—

CLARITY

*Hold breath. Close eyes. Keep eyes closed till
crimson glow appears on underside of eyelid,
replacing customary black. Still holding breath,
concentrate on nothingness (black space void
before universe existed), and fill black space up,
fast as possible, with:*

A. *Whirling silver flecks coagulate.*

B. *Aerial goobers.*

C. *Goobers build up into globs.*

D. *First rain.*

E. *Mucky ooze.*

F. *Amoeba.*

G. *Small lizard suns itself on flat stone.*

H. *Armadillo trail in muck creates deep
and fertile valley, shaded by
overhangs from perpetual sunlight.*

I. *Roaches hang on for dear life on giraffe.*

J. *Amoeba: six feelers.*

K. *Amoeba stands erect.*

L. *Roaches fall off giraffe.*

M. *Amoeba eats fruit.*

N. *Changes in brain-cells. Sees "dust."*

O. *Dust-storm. Retreat into cave.*

P. *Memory of dream: chase. Feelers tingle.*

Q. *Laughs at antics of roaches trying to
clamber on giraffe—big flood.*

R. *Amoeba decides to fly.*

S. *Auk.*
T. *Humanoid head pops out of ooze.*
U. *Wings drop off amoeba.*
V. *Feelers drop off.*
W. *Globs disintegrate into goobers.*
X. *Aerial goobers. Vanish.*
Y. *Silver flecks disintegrate.*
Z. *Whirling slows down, stops.*

Take a breath. Open eyes. Rest a little.

3. CONQUER THIRD LIFE OBSTACLE—

POWER

*Stare at "Native Innards" box. Wait for box to
look normal—no glowing, no favorite color. Don't
boss it, let it do work. When box looks really
normal, like kitchen appliance, or coat hanging in
closet—focus on what's going on outside
eye-shaped window. Don't get up to look out.
If strong notion of what's going on outside, get
up fast from Chain of Being spot and check it
out. If correct, return, wait for next notion.
Repeat. Check it out. Repeat. Check it out. If
second or third notion is incorrect (right person,
wrong companion—right car, wrong passenger,
right companion, wrong direction) better return
to protozoic blob state and hunt for right position
in Evolution Cosmos. May have shifted in interim.
Safer procedure is to start over from scratch.
Probably haven't conquered all fears yet—night,
war, death, starvation, poverty, disease, Hell, old
age, the Government, insanity, murder, all alone,
abandoned, lost, no way out, life sentence.*

perversions, black magic, return of youth and
innocence—power.

I got to be so proficient at correct sightings, I became
suspicious. What if my new knack were due to sounds
(chugs, taps, bangs) drifting up through the eye-shaped
attic window? I took to putting wads of cotton in my
ears, which actually hurried things along considerably by
eliminating distracting outside interferences (door chimes,
sportscasts, distant wrist alarms of doctors hurrying
towards appointments). My three favorite correct sightings
were (covering a three-month period):

1. Mr. Lindley on his way to his law office.
   Straw hat, blazer, mustachio. Open car.
   "Spanish Suez" I thought it was, thanks to
   Mummers. Musical horn played *Dreaming of
   Snow*, which Mr. Lindley'd sing:

   > *Dreaming of Snow*
   > *I missed you last week*
   > *Dreaming of Snow*
   > *I missed all you speak*
   > *Of.*

   > *Little things like skol,*
   > *Our wishing well, orange bowl,*
   > *The time our "teepees"*
   > *Tangled in the trees,*
   > *You were such a tease*
   > *I fell upon my knees,*
   > *Love.*

   > *Dreaming of Snow,*
   > *Each crystal unique.*
   > *Dreaming of—*

Never heard how it ended. And never really
got the right word for "teepees."

2. Sam Choon's red laundry truck.

3. Motorcade of family of Hungarian-Jewish-Nagas
who lived across the street in a bunch
of stucco bungalows hidden behind a Buddha
Lying Down berry hedge. Money came from
turban wrapping machine invention—use
spread rapidly from Sikh laundries and
monastic groups to private homes throughout
the Orient and N. P. Region. So uppity, they
each had their own individual limousine and
chauffeur—deemed it abhorrent invasion of
privacy to sit with any passenger other than
babe in arms of same sex—momentous
processions, leave for factory at any hour—
confabs.

Back to my ritual. The important, final conquest:

4. CONQUER FOURTH LIFE OBSTACLE—

OLD AGE

*Stare at "Native Innards" box, after a minimum
of three correct sightings, or more—if not feeling
steady and content inside, with sense of inner
balance, being at right place at right time. If
OK, get old glow going, plus favorite color—OK
to blink, breathe, burp, fart—whatever's natural.
Hard part starts. Keep eyes blinking normally,
and at same time, focus on memory glimpse of
"Dog Roots" girl, revolving and revolving; edge*

memory from eyelid underside onto attic surfaces
—canoe with hole in one side, porch swing with
monogrammed "M & E & B," ebony riverboat
spittoon, etc. edge memory glimpse from
surfaces towards "Native Innards" box.
Now comes tricky part. Get memory glimpse
of "Dog Roots" girl to melt (still revolving and
revolving) into side of box. Gather as many
memory glimpses of "Dog Roots" girl, keeping
them identical, as possible, edging each one into
the box, placing it inside so as not to bump into
out-of-visual-range previous "Dog Roots" girls,
revolving and revolving in box, letting this new
in-the-box awareness carry one along, without
fear, without delusion one is gifted with clarity
(like everything, comes and goes), with power
nuttiness (watch, don't try to control), and if
"Dog Roots" girls parade out attic window,
bumping into each other, scratching at each other,
shouting obscenities, let them, and also avoid fear
of time running out, of aging as each girl
revolves (more vision may mean speed quickens
due to greater awareness of time), with death
staring one in the face, and nothing much to
remember. Accept fact these memory glimpses
are not actual. Keep going until attain ecstasy.
Then exhaustion. Ecstasy of exhaustion—whirling
slows down, stops . . .

I felt something bosomy pressing against me. It was so
late at night, I knew Mummers was fast asleep, either that,
or prowling in search of a new Mummy Adventure in
the false city, where girls from the backwoods, or so he

told me, whispered in the shadows, "Nirvana juice for sale, Jungle Jim Babe juices for the handsome gent, make you double he-man, swell mister!"—and knowingly, they'd lead him to their Jungle Jim Babe, a freckled young 'un fresh from the pine mountains, before whom Mummers'd arch himself into his favorite auto position, by now naked and sweaty, arms curved like front fenders, legs intertwined grasshopper-style (rear bumper)—or so he'd tell me the following morning at breakfast, savoring each detail—how the Jungle Jim Babe had given him a shine with a chamois cloth provided him by Mummers (a cloth with quite a history) until, after an indeterminate period of feeling gentle circular motions, Mummers' body'd start quivering (speeding sensation), thrusting violently (flying off cliff into soft earth), then the gratification instant (fatal crash!)—after which Mummers would pay the Jungle Jim Babe for some stolen good or other taken caressingly out of a carton yanked from under the bed (golden faucet with dragon's mouth spout, actually a worthless plastic composite; illegal Swiss "virility" pills, harmless placebos; Coptic Cross of St. Rita, genuine mother-of-pearl, actually macaroni and dried okra wedges sprayed with glitter-dust), make his adieus, tipping the backwoods girls, then, while waiting for a streetcar, Mummers'd memorize the encounter thoroughly, the better to regale me with the following morning—

Thinking something had gone kerflooey with my inner balance, I zipped all the way back from OLD AGE to FEAR, which meant canceling out two totally correct sightings:

1. A burly woman in a Farmer Jones hat,
   sprawled on a tractor, one hand on its wheel,
   using the other to swig from a beer can.
   Attached to the tractor was a covered wagon

with "YANKEE DAY" written on its side.
Musket-and-pumpkin motif on tarpaulin. She
was singing, at the top of her lungs, a
patriotic rouser:

Beaming we glow,
I hissed you, past clique.
Beaming we glow,
I list all you reek
    Of.

Riddle jinx like goal,
And hushing hell—Foreign Soul.
The crime is "free bees"
Hanging in the breeze,
We were in a squeeze,
Till you made your decrees,
    Love.

Beaming we glow,
Yes, week after week.
Beaming we glow—

Never heard how it ended. And never really
got the right word for "free bees."

2. Second tractor driven by heavy-set
bronze-skinned man in tux—I recognized him
as one of the Hungarian-Jewish-Nagas.
Attached to his tractor was a wagon, and on
it—a huge white turban made of styrofoam.
All up and down it, in little holes, one could
see gangly hillbilly faces, men, none too
happy looking. Attached to the apex of the
turban was the slogan:

Beaming We The Foremen Glow!

A group of tall and gangly women in poke bonnets and pioneer dresses jog-trotted along grimly, alongside the turban float, holding aloft a banner of toilet-paper roses:

Beaming We The Receptionists Glow!

Kit and kaboodle, the two tractors and jog-trotters turned into the driveway, and proceeded side by side past the Buddha Lying Down hedge. Factory celebration? Incentive fiesta?

I felt the bosomy pressing again. I craned around. A red tag was stuck to my shoulder, with one word on it:

DESTROY

I looked up. It was the "Dog Roots" girl, leaning against me. In a blue serge suit with white gloves. Two words were emblazoned on a green ribbon that encircled the brim of her cowboy hat:

ENVIRONMENT COMPTROLLER

I wanted to embrace her, to kneel in front of her, and unzip her suit. Mummers was standing beside her, whispering to her. She was watching me, bemusedly, while paying attention to what he was saying. She nodded, and tore a tag out of a small book that hung from her belt. She licked it, and stuck it on my other shoulder. It said:

FIX

She was laughing, laughing away. Inside her mouth, I noticed gold fillings. Her neck had creases. She wore face powder. Her mouth curved downwards, even when laughing, and two hard lines led from her mouth down to her chin. The first chin. Then came the second one that wobbled when she laughed. She had an old lady body odor, like sweet gas. Gray wisps were stuck to her neck, which bulged. Her wig was tilted. She was wheezing.

I must have screamed, judging from the look Mummers gave me, as he ushered her towards the west wing, through an arch. I watched as they ambled down the attic corridor, stopping here and there to tag an object. They disappeared behind a standing mirror. Without knowing why I did what I did, I got up, grabbed the "Native Innards" box, pried open the fire trapdoor that led to my bedroom below, and dropped the box, watching it land on my bed. I shut the trapdoor, and returned to my Chain of Being spot. I took the wads of cotton out of my ears. The Chain of Being spot felt like any spot for anyone. I could hear steps, ripping sounds, pause, then a thwack: tagging.

Clack of boots on attic stairs: it was safe to look up. She was behind Mummers. First step: she was ankleless. Mummers? All head. Second step: legs cut off at knees. No more Mummers. Third step. Amputated at thighs.

Fourth step. Lower half of sex area plus rest of her cut off. Fifth step. Axed in middle of stomach. Sixth step. Nice statue effect. Classical bust. Seventh step. Sculpture of head with piece of shoulder from old ruin. Eighth step. Decapitated head floating in harsh crimson light, pulsating. Ninth step. Cowboy hat, floating on its own, plus upper half of ribbon word:

COMPTROLLER

"Dog Roots" girls swarm over it, revolving and revolving, batter hat, dive-bomb it. Pause. Tenth step. No one. Army of revolving and revolving "Dog Roots" girls, falls to floor, flaccid thumps, blobs, no one.

Right then and there, I gave up any idea of pursuing *The Yankee Way of Knowledge* any further. I just wasn't cut out to be A Man of Knowledge.

Happy to be free of my arduous ritual, I strolled about the attic, no longer confined to my Chain of Being spot. Everywhere, there were tags:

SELL

GOV'T

AS IS

FIX

DESTROY

I felt something bosomy pressing against me. Mummers. I was sitting under the eye-shaped window, where the "Native Innards" box had been. He was carrying a pink plastic doll-house, shaped like a pyramid. He asked me to move, and he set it down, where I had been sitting.

The doll-house contained six miniature rooms, three on the ground floor, two on the second, and one on the third. I recalled how proudly he'd exhibited it to me—a souvenir brought back from one of his Jungle Jim Babe escapades in the false city back of the factory gulch, an escapade that had several Mummyish highlights—hand with pointed fingernails rakes back like five roadsters all going out of control in race—

Instead of the domestic scenes one might expect, the rooms illustrated an important moment in the lives of six explorers:

GROUND FLOOR

1. Micholitz	2. Forster	3. Roebling
Tanen-tuang-gyi Mountains. Leg dangling over a black abyss. On rope bridge, he sits.	Pacucha Valley. Eats avocado—sand. Sad mule. Stares at face reflection in sand.	Guaíra Falls. Takes a shower in them. Men with tooth tattoos peer from vines.

SECOND FLOOR

4. Osmers	5. Arnold
Lago de Maracaibo. Skiff.	Surigao Plateau. Poisoned stakes.

THIRD FLOOR

6. Warscewicz
Hills of Nirgu.

Mummers told me, "Hey boy . . . looked all over for
it . . . 'Native Innards' box . . . not in attic . . . upset
. . . DESTROY . . . she left . . . found it on your bed
. . . in basement . . . hid it in trunk tagged AS IS . . .
leave it behind, boy . . . never think of it again . . . as a
parting gift . . . The Six Explorer Pyramid . . . Young
'Un told me of rubies in the sand . . . diamonds woven
into the rope bridge . . . sapphires behind the falls . . .
take it on your journey, boy . . . on your own now
. . . many rivers . . . many cities . . . to a place of
. . . of . . . godspeed, boy . . . hey boy . . . only take
paths that have art . . . orchids in the sand . . . orchids
woven in the rope bridge . . . orchids behind the falls
. . . only challenge is to traverse each path to its end . . .
looking breathlessly."

He removed the red tags from my shoulders, and stuck
them on his own:

DESTROY

On the left one. On the right one:

FIX

My first path, he informed me, would begin ". . . in a
land . . . flat as a pancake . . . and flowerless, flowerless!"

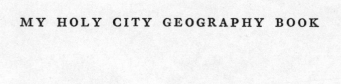

MY HOLY CITY GEOGRAPHY BOOK

ROUNDING THE LEAF!
SAFELY ON MY WAY!
ROUNDING THE LEAF!

That's how I started each day at Blue Institute. Tired of greasy spoon joints, hitching across asphalt mesas, listening to rickety sofa-beds and freight-cars shunting in the night (banana trains), I was only too happy to be a full-fledged Junior at Blue Institute. First thing every morning, rain or shine, I'd sit up in my genuine Civil War hospital bed, and shout it out, loud and clear—

ROUNDING THE LEAF!
SAFELY ON MY WAY!
ROUNDING THE LEAF!

Jan—March (first leaf)
Apr—Jun (second leaf)
July—Sept (third leaf)
Oct—Dec (fourth leaf)

ROUNDING THE LEAF!
SAFELY ON MY WAY!
ROUNDING THE LEAF!

I'd based my style of living quarters on a nineteenth-century Yankee hospital room, which I modeled on a photograph—part of a foto-essay about Walt Whitman and his war experiences as a male nurse. The photograph showed a cubicle, and in it, Walt Whitman sitting on a chair, head cocked sideways, beard tilted sideways, holding a pad tilted sideways in his lap—evidently snoozing. A youth, wearing a kepi, but bare-chested, was lying in bed, reading a newspaper tilted sideways. The only words I could make out were "moon," "futures," "massacre," "weevil," "junction," "barn," "swathe," "scabbard," "war," "fife," "insult," "gin," "slavery," and "disguised in female garb, the President of the Confederacy made his—"

ROUNDING THE LEAF!
SAFELY ON MY WAY!
ROUNDING THE LEAF!

> *Jan—March (first leaf)*
> *Apr—Jun (second leaf)*
> *July—Sept (third leaf)*
> *Oct—Dec (fourth leaf)*

ROUNDING THE LEAF!
SAFELY ON MY WAY!
ROUNDING THE LEAF!

My living quarters consisted of hospital bed, aforementioned, plus a washstand (replica of soldier's) beside it (basin, water pitcher, towel racks) plus a three-sectioned screen (replica of soldier's) made of cheesecloth which I unfolded when I felt a "Holy City Seizure" coming on —more about that later. In my washstand, in the potty compartment, I placed a replica of Walt Whitman I'd painstakingly whittled out of pine, and coated with plastic. I used my increasingly luxuriant pubic bush for his beard, tweaking each hair out, hair by hair, glueing each one on, one by one. By exposing myself to the winter sun (mirrors, ribbons of flesh), I collected enough acne-free skin-strips to coat the face and hands area. For his eyes, tapioca balls, tinted blue. Nostril hairs, down from my arms.

ROUNDING THE LEAF!
SAFELY ON MY WAY!
ROUNDING THE LEAF!

Jan—March (first leaf)
Apr—Jun (second leaf)
July—Sept (third leaf)
Oct—Dec (fourth leaf)

ROUNDING THE LEAF!
SAFELY ON MY WAY!
ROUNDING THE LEAF!

This was my way of trying to fit into Blue Institute, which had been founded during the Civil War by a scion of the famous Blue Family of comic artists, to provide a training ground for young lads who sought to unravel the secrets of laughter. The aims of the Institute soon widened. What was the link between "laughter" and "history"? Soon the "City" was added. Which altered, via usage, to "Holy City," and from there to "Holy City Geography."

ROUNDING THE LEAF!
SAFELY ON MY WAY!
ROUNDING THE LEAF!

Jan–March (first leaf)
Apr–Jun (second leaf)
July–Sept (third leaf)
Oct–Dec (fourth leaf)

ROUNDING THE LEAF!
SAFELY ON MY WAY!
ROUNDING THE LEAF!

I added one personal touch, a tray that could be raised and lowered from the ceiling by a pulley system neatly tucked behind a false wall behind the bed. I did all my studying, in bed, on this tray. Thus the staff and student body gathered that I was a somewhat special case, and they oughtn't to demand total submission to the Blue Institute regulations meant for average, up-and-about Blue Institute students.

ROUNDING THE LEAF!
SAFELY ON MY WAY!
ROUNDING THE LEAF!

ROUNDING THE LEAF!
SAFELY ON MY WAY!
ROUNDING THE LEAF!

Just like a cloverleaf traffic pattern—that's how we were taught to visualize how rounding the leaf progress works—continuous flow maintained—never gets out of hand—always something moving day and night—if 51% of the population (5,000,000 or over) (adults) rounded the leaf—everyone would have optimum—far as we got—

ROUNDING THE LEAF!
SAFELY ON MY WAY!
ROUNDING THE LEAF!

A runner in a nineteenth-century photographic study of motion—that's how we were taught to visualize rounding the leaf progress in terms of the individual psyche. In terms of his life, "rounding the leaf awareness provides the individual and/or his psyche with a series of inter-connected configurations, eventually forming a corolla, irregular but personate, a corolla which shrouds one inside a permanent energy field, until one's body has totally and painlessly disintegrated—at which point the corolla—"

That's as far as we ever got, but rounding the leaf awareness became a basic bulwark to me at this juncture. I soon forgot my attic pleasures and rituals, and I left Mummers' parting gift in my foot-locker in the gym. Explorers were no concern of mine.

Our only textbook, if it can be called that, was "Holy City Geography Book." Not that my rounding the leaf awareness was intensified by its actual text—far from it! Oof, the Holy City geographies we skipped! Tayasal, Thebes, Byzantium, Harappa, Mohenjo-Daro, each with its own labyrinths and other holy structures, thrusting sideways and upwards and sometimes downwards, often squeezing the faces of saints and idols into stony grimaces misleading to those who peer into the eyes of such statues in search of—who knows? Happy New Year times?

Chapter Fifteen of "Holy City Geography Book"— "Rome in the Dark Ages"—consumed the better part of the school year. There was little time left for the other Holy Cities. We spent the entire fall term building Rome's basic temples and barracks and marketplaces according to detailed blueprints in the text. We utilized refuse procured from the local small-town dump, such as it was—mostly rusty lubricating oil cans, tires, and scraps of automobiles discarded from various automobile graveyards outside the town limits. Blue Town boasted a turnpike full of hairpin curves, adequately paved but badly graded; there was little traffic except in autumn, when the beet farmers could be seen carrying their produce to market, inching along, trucks piled high with their teetering blood-red harvest, so high, whole stacks of beets fell at each curve, rendering it dangerously slippery. Ensuing trucks had to really inch along, giving the first few trucks an edge at the distribution center in the next county; they raked in the profits, and by the time the slowpokes arrived, the market was glutted—and we knew we were in for weeks of beet-loaf, beet jello, beet soup, beet salad, beet juice, beet shakes, beet shreds, beet wedges, beet mounds, beet casseroles, beet stews, beet salads, and just plain cooked beets!

Often we were commandeered to mop up the road; afterwards, muscles aching, we'd gather in the local roadhouse (an Illusion House was reputed to be on the second floor, and it's true, the shades were always down on those windows, all day long)—and we'd listen to the beet farmers tell highway jokes, about drunken truckers lying down on the county road. Their wives are summoned, and seeing their husbands all gory, assume there's been an invasion, or something—monsters from Mars, enemy shock troops! The truckers get up, howling at their wives' ashen faces. The wives conk out, like bowling pins, they're so surprised! Out cold on the highway, the wives, getting gory too. The story continues, and, skipping to the end, the punch line is:

"I thought you were a GONER, Rhea!"

One of the wives is named Rhea, and it comes up earlier in the joke, a good ways back, before the highway part, the breakfast part—from one bungalow to the next—it

comes up that she's the town slut. She's been sleeping with
the road commissioner (he accuses her, justly, of "copro-
philia"—she snaps right back, "Never slept with a dick
in my life!"), the high school principal (he accuses her,
justly, of "coprophilia"—she snaps right back, "Never
slept with a dick in my life!"), and the proprietors of the
local filling station, father and son (they accuse her, justly
and jointly, of "coprophilia"—she snaps right back, "So
I've slept with a dick, but his name ain't Phil!"), mean-
while keeping her husband, the local sanitation officer,
sexually satisfied.

These slippery highway stories must have cut down on
local traffic considerably, and what traffic there was, was
painfully slow—hence few crashes. Our Rome in the
Dark Ages was woefully lacking in the chrome depart-
ment.

Upon our return from Christmas vacation, we were
geared to cover fifty years of Roman Holy City Geog-
raphy a week—a healthy clip, excellent for developing
our rounding the leaf awareness. In an average week, say,
we'd raze blocks of imperial palaces and build barracks
for the German barbarian chieftains and their Slavic con-
cubine armies on Monday, say, fire in the slave quarters,
Tuesday, say, Wednesday, no class, Thursday, say, we'd
dig a canal under a full moon—ragged loonies that we
were—to rid the city of the mosquito menace (Papal
Edict) by draining the swamps (more about the full moon
—i.e., Diana Vienna—later), and Friday, say, we'd tear
down the Slavic concubine barracks and convert them
into gigantic pleasure baths, honeycombed with rooms
for youths, youths and maidens, leaders, the sick, the aged,
the dark, the foreign, the poor, the mad. Schedules were
worked out so that each individual, shunted about by

pulleys and slides with gentle downward slopes, sampled each and every room—except us magicians, who were relegated to secret rooms in order to prophesy the city's future by "reading the steam." In separate rooms, we lay down and spoke into innertube mouthpieces, relating our "reading the steam" prophecies to seniors, who took everything down faithfully, and correlated the prophecies into an organic whole: the Holy City Geography of Rome, i.e.—its future. I improvised a crude bed out of two halved oil drums laid end to end. Oil rags served as a mattress—a fender was my pillow. I'd lie down and reach for my innertube coil, and begin dredging for prophecies, all the while looking for puffs of steam that inched their way across the gymnasium ceiling—actually clouds made by a sonic theatre machine manipulated by our teacher, Miss Hinckle. Why she chose me as magician I'll never know, but I can guess why my senior was Diana Vienna. She was a blond six-footer, Diana was, with hair down to her waist, and she wore oil-cloth map dresses of her own devising. The maps were always of Vienna Through the Ages—beautifully lettered in Gothic script: Franz Josef Strasse, Bahnhof, Stat-Oper, the parks green, the cathedrals mauve, the avenues and principal thoroughfares black. How she loved Vienna's "dusty imperial corners"—ergo, her nickname. I noticed her first when I saw her hoisted into position as moon the day we dug the canal. We were foreign workmen, rather disturbed by this enforced labor, and at the sight of her legs flailing above us, painted gold, with her face jewel-encrusted, we went bonkers. We shoveled, scooped earth with our bare hands, formed lickety-split chains—our guards scratched their heads. We were clearly men possessed! And when the canal was finished, hours ahead of schedule, we waited for her to be lowered into our arms, in the vain belief she would lead us to a city in the sky where we could be free, and forever young—gods. Instead, she was cranked higher and higher, and she vanished into a trapdoor that silently opened and closed. She disappeared behind sudden threatening clouds. Something spiraled down. I fell on it. Bodies fell on me. I gasped for air. The crushing weight grew lighter. Only one figure lay on top of me, pressed against me, his arms around my stomach. An unshaven jaw jabbed my neck. I looked up: a guard. Barry Wingate was his name. He yanked off my work pants. To prepare us for the outside world, each day, a different sex mores guidance sheet was posted, ranging from "abstinence" to just about everything under the sun. The day we dug the canal, the choices were as follows:

1.   Imbue article of clothing with sexuality.
2.   Submission to higher-up—same sex only.
3.   Gather crowd. Performance.

I took off my underwear, obligingly. As I expected, Barry Wingate went, "Ugh!" That morning, I'd painted several chancres on my rear, painstakingly copied from a medical book.

I sat up. I was alone. I opened my hand, and saw a small turquoise, shaped like an orchid. I balanced it on the tip of my erect penis.

When the next Sweet-On Day rolled around, I dedicated a dance to Diana Vienna. I came out on the auditorium stage in a parka, heavily bundled up, with snowshoes on. I stamped my feet, and went, "Brrr! Brrr!" I launched into a tap-dance that, much to my chagrin, had the audience in stitches. An ominous violet dusk darkened the stage (thanks to Barry Wingate, who was manipulating the sonic theatre machine). Wolves howled. Winds whined, growing in intensity until they were seemingly out of control, able to scoop up roofs, flatten cities. A penguin (huge projection) entered and stood surveying me, then exited. The stage tilted gradually, and, as I clawed its sheer surface, luminous black waters (sonic projection again) rose waist-high. A round plaster moon rapidly descended. Lunging up from my "iceberg," I grasped the moon with one hand, and soared upward, clinging as it rose. My snowshoes and fur pants, my parka and thermal scarf fell to the stage, one by one, followed by my underwear, wrist-watch, sox, and dark glasses. Naked in mid-air, I opened a small door in the plaster moon, with my free hand. Imitation diamonds and rubies poured into my mouth. End of scene.

After the curtains had closed, and as I was falling towards the waiting net, I heard Miss Hinckle in the auditorium shouting, "Beast! Beast!"—with hysterical intensity. Upon asking Barry why she was so insulting, he informed me what *BIS* meant.

What a wild look Miss Hinckle gave me when she announced the next day that Diana Vienna had been appointed my prophecy collator.

Jan—March (first leaf)
Apr—Jun (second leaf)
July—Sept (third leaf)
Oct—Dec (fourth leaf)

January: "rounding the leaf." Prophecies.
February: "rounding the leaf." Prophecies.
March: "rounding the leaf." Prophecies.
I tried to read the steam, impersonally, like an efficient conduit, tried to focus on future population components,

the Vatican's marble input, replacement of monuments that are worn away by the kisses of the devout, rodent control, parks, refrigeration, sewerage, sewerage used on vegetable fields, old people's homes, vaults, the virginal air, couples making love under the Tiber bridges, sex laws, child molesters, gigolos, oiling up one's body:

> *the American magician will slide down a hill of Vienna*
>   *breasts*
> *wetting each one with tongue and sweat until he arrests*
> *girls parading through Rome's moony mind*
> *with great thighs and juices and thighs,*
> *till a mortar pounds watermelon. Scooped out. Rind.*
> *The nature of its pink, if asserted, buys—*

My prophecies invariably took an unabashed sexual turn, and Diana Vienna'd start to moan in her distant cubicle up above. Driblets of spittle'd fall out of the innertube mouthpiece onto my waiting stomach and thighs. Often I'd shake it violently in the hopes of getting more juices from the moon (ha!), but there never was enough, and so I was driven to self-anointing, or else whole areas of my body would have remained parched. Besides, as the French say, what is love but the mixture of two salivas? Three salivas, in this case, for often Barry Wingate would sneak into my secret room, and lie next to me, sharing the juices. One day, blood trickled out, enough to smear my whole chest and buttocks, with enough left over to anoint Barry's face. I heard sobbing coming through the mouthpiece. I fell asleep. When I woke up, it was late afternoon, and time to watch the traffic turn red from the sunset. I ran to the assembly, with its picture window overlooking the three-lane county road. There in the senior balcony was my Diana, with bandaged wrists, staring at me icily. Fragments welled up: wet oil rags, a vein throbs in my forehead—thirstiness—her tongue is on my stomach now—above her—manipulate between my—swelling—her lips part—fake "Holy City Seizure"?—peeing out pleasantly, then a painful jab—stabbed hairy spider contracts, all its legs curling in and in as blood trickles over the black hairy surface with six-legged white lice scurrying out of the path of the lava flood—

I concentrated on the county road. A blue sedan went by, dented rear fender, farmer's son driving: tow-headed. Then: pickup truck. Black man. Black truck. The hour was up: two vehicles.

The following day, I read the steam to Diana Vienna calmly and impersonally. Barry Wingate was not present. We filled three notebooks, a record for us. The prophecies dealt with certain merchandising problems—specifically how to deal with the spoilage rate of imported vegetables, fruit, and meat. Aqueducts, enough ice to last through the summer, prices . . .

More notebooks—statues, their placement and upkeep. The regularization of traffic, so that a prelate, leaving his dwelling for a conference, eight years since the last one, encounters, say, the hunchback asleep, being shaken awake by the Ethiopian, as before; it is his turn to throw the dice and he'll win, as he did eight years before. The same red-headed slattern is hugging the farmer's fat mother . . . she collapses, dead drunk . . . bugs in the dusk light . . . sudden agitation . . . lawns go uncut . . . explosions . . . the gypsy child . . . foresees auto crash . . . exactly like eight years before . . . the smokestack buckles . . . the graffiti on the cobblestone in blue chalk . . . it's in Arabic . . . next to a mathematical problem involving a distribution formula involving imported wine—

While Miss Hinckle knew better than to force us past reading the steam into the inevitable Sack of Rome (which we voted to skip)—in the middle of April, we voted to move on—to Mecca. Using sheets, we constructed winding alleys through the buildings and dyed ourselves brown. The seniors, veiled on ladders, peered down at us hostilely, making clicking noises with their tongues. Tommies disguised as Pilgrims, we marched to the mosque (bio lab) and smashed the bottles (Allah)—at which point the tower bells chimed:

ROUNDING THE LEAF!
SAFELY ON MY WAY!
ROUNDING THE LEAF!

Spring Vacation!

At the railway station, peering by chance into a roomette, I saw a man in a bowler hat, sitting beside Diana Vienna, who was wearing dark glasses. Her wrists were bandaged and she was lying down on the lower berth, facing the window, with a nightgown on, with yellow full moons on it repeated against a skyscraper background. The man shook his fist at me. His lips were working away as the train pulled out of the station.

I waited till nightfall for the next express.

Upon our return, Barry Wingate sat in Diana Vienna's place in the senior balcony.

Until Commencement, all through the spring term, Miss

Hinckle read us selections from the gibberish dream books of oldsters of the Shaker persuasion, Shakers whose condominiums in Maine and New England hardly constituted cities in the accepted sense of the word, clearly an out-of-whack tolerance installation attempt (oldsters, virginity, gnarled rhapsody) which fooled no one.

During our last class with Miss Hinckle, something odd happened to me. She began, out of the blue, to "cartoon" on me—i.e., "Holy City Seizure." White blobs on her rosy cheeks reflected an apple on her desk. The apple had white blobs that reflected my face—I was in the first row, and, in fact, had given her the apple. Her pendant earrings began swaying, like grandfather clock pendulums, as she peered over her spectacles. Her hand jerked down towards the desk and opened a book. A fly landed on the page, and walked across it. It climbed on her finger, and sat on her diamond wedding ring. A second fly landed on the first, and mounted it. I could see the thrusts. She cleared her throat reprovingly. The flies reversed positions. More thrusts. She began wagging her finger at the flies, who scooted off. Then she wagged her finger at me, why I couldn't imagine. Something about "rude to stare"? I worried about her being an imposter—how come the ring? *Miss* Hinckle? Her voice again: IF YOU DON'T RESPOND, I HAVE NO RECOURSE BUT TO LEAVE!

Terrible cartoon. I remember wondering why she didn't go. Soon enough, her voice lulled me, as she began reading her favorite Shaker Dream Book Exchange Dream. One often saw it, in those days, in gas station rest-rooms, or folded inside supermarket throwaway newspapers with lists of the day's bargains. She'd made us learn it by heart, four lines per day, and soon we chimed in:

. . . thing happens to us in Black Hills, S.D.
we stop in Mission, S.D. to buy redhots
for ice-cream sandwiches in dry ice in hamper
and stop at a wayside just outside Mission.

We want to set and eat so the kids can have a
change, though Ruby's happy counting telephone
poles, and Howie's busy counting his favorite
auto, the La Salle (eighteen by noon and he

wouldn't sneeze at owning one, Dream Book) and
Old Suntan has his nose out the window, guess what?
The doors are locked on the Supermarket. Then
they see we're from out-of-state and let us in.

Ole Mole Minzy two
Acren, makren, way knee view.
Ho-a, oh-a, play with you.
Ole zello, woo-woo-woo.

Such a nice thing for those sweet checkers
to go and do. Now guess what? You bet we get
home safe but guess what? Go on, don't care
if you're J. P. Morgan or whoever, stop making

yourself miserable thinking about your troubles,
if that's what you're up to—your job, figure,
gittin' old, moolah givin' out, doc bills, hubby punk,
cleans his fingernails on bible page corners,

puts his snot on the undersides of tables and chairs
for Suntan to lick up, scrapes his tongue with his
fingernails when no one's lookin' (HE thinks!) and
eats the stuff we used to call tongue jam in high

balls of sippy puppy joy
Ho-a, oh-a, hoi polloi.
Acren, makren, fat foo foy,
Ole zello, boy-oh-boy.

school guessed what yet? Nope? Then guess I'd
better level with you folks. Can't find my front-door
key, that's what. So just for a joke I knock on the door
and sing out, "Anybody home?" Here's the surprise!

Those supermarket checkers let us in! See, I'd
dropped my address book right by the checkout counter
reaching for my purse, and my address book was in it,
with my address in pencil on the end paper.

A sassy Jesus surprise! I said a sassy Jesus surprise!
Key'd fallen out too. And that's the how-come-of-it-all,
the sassy Jesus surprise. And now we all grab hands
and I don't know what-all and dance around rejoicing.

Co ho haw hooh huh huh haw
Co ho haw hooh huh huh paw
Co ho haw hooh huh huh jaw
Co ho haw hooh huh huh haw

And we lie down and soon flowers and leaves and
pollen and stalks are entering our mouths
and passing out our front places
and end places

passing from one to another
not gittin' dirtied in any way,
just passin' from one to 'tuther,
in and out our various human openings

from one to 'tuther
in silence.

Passing from one to 'tuther
in silence.

Heh, hae it, will ye hae it?
Tanderan vanderan try it
valve valve buy it
vak vaj dry it

From on to 'tuther
in silence.
Passing from one to 'tuther
in silence.

A great and wondrous
quiet unity
whooshed through me
as nice as a sassy feather with a mind of its own,

That licks and sniffs like a puppy, Dream Book.
Arose refreshed to find Supermarket people
gone and a note on the pincushion:
Enjoyed visit. Goodbye. Anyone from out there . . .

Saved by the bell. My "Holy City Seizure" stopped.
The smell of fresh-cut grass welled up through the puri-
fier vents. The chair was sticky. I was sweating. My "Holy
City Seizure" was over. I ran out of the room, without
saying goodbye to Miss Hinckle, without even looking
at her ring finger. I hurried down corridor after corridor,
speeding past windows that looked out on a quadrangle.
I thought I saw someone racing along the opposite side of
the quadrangle, on the same floor I was, hurrying from
window to window—like me.

I wasn't sure where I was heading until: there it was—
my oil-drum bed. For the first time since Diana Vienna's

departure, I reached up and touched the mouthpiece, dangling there. After a while, I calmed down—my "Holy City Seizure" (spinny sensation, end of the world feeling) was really over—no cartooning. I opened my "Holy City Geography Book" in search of the next move guidance. I didn't seem to be safely on my way, rounding the leaf, not by a long shot. I stared at the end-papers, which I'd never really noticed before.

What a feast!

"HOLY CITY GEOGRAPHY BOOK" END-PAPER

THE SKY

1. UPPER SKY

A. *Huge dirigible. Passengers peering out of
    observation booth windows, front and back.
    They are all Orientals.*

B. *Sliver of sun barely visible just above
    dirigible's upper edge—jagged fin protrusions.
    Light rays radiate outward in crude "rising
    sun" newspaper cartoon style.*

2. MIDDLE SKY

A. *Four groups of monoplanes in "V" formation,
    heading outwards in four directions, forming
    a rectangle. I once had called these
    monoplanes "an airplane sandwich" within
    earshot of Miss Hinckle. Just a joke, so I
    thought, but from then on, I was fair game
    for merciless teasing (her instigation)—"Have
    some choo-choo pie"—railroad terminal;
    "putt-putt junket"—lake dock. You see, at
    recess, we'd "eat the city," standing around
    a big board with model houses, traffic cubes,
    bushes, etc. Everything was real food. You
    see, environmental engorgement was in its
    heyday as a weapon against passive-aggressive
    foetal "shirk" fugue reactions—veins of
    womb, their blueness, transposed into traffic
    streams, longing to "cordon it off"
    (strangulation—snip off umbilical cord
    prematurely), then longing to dent surfaces,
    paint them "good as new" (little resurrection
    ritual), lick them to heal them (atonement),
    tongue all cut, swells up, turns black
    (strangulation by self)—the color one dies is
    the color one is reborn—safely on way, etc.*

B. *Mail plane.*

3. LOWER SKY

    A. *Sack dropping from mail plane.*

    B. *Group of postmen on stilts form a circle around what could be practice net for acrobats.*

    C. *Roughnecks in trees. Ammunition belts. Machine guns camouflaged to look like greenery.*

4. HORIZON

A.   *Ten-lane super-highway layered so as to
form a traffic cube, with lots of time to
coast at 150 mph—top layer wending its
way past vast factory roofs with great
brand-names slanted towards the sun.*

B.   *One touch of darkness. Delicate black lines,
like tendrils of a vine, moving outward
from a series of headlights. As sun is shining,
this is device to show viewer headlights
are on in broad daylight. Rear third of
flower-laden limousine preceding headlights
visible. Rest hidden behind luxurious mobile
home in the slow-lane (trucks etc.).*

C.   *Middle-aged couple eat breakfast on what
is fixed up to be minute patio (rear-end
of mobile home). In their bathing suits.
Chauffeur does driving up front. Stares
straight ahead, ignores cortege passing in
lane beside them (limousine etc.).*

D.   *Cortege consists of omnibus for immediate
family (first), then station wagons for intimate
friends, phaeton sedans for relatives, coupes
for work colleagues and employees, then open
trucks for those tangentially affected, and
finally the human touch: a rumbleseat with a
moppet on it cuddling a chihuahua. NO ONE*

in front-seat. Some kind of viewer test, trick
of hack artist to see if anyone's paying
attention, still waiting for someone somewhere
to write in: SIR! NO ONE in front seat,
suggest . . .

E. Anyway, traffic system working in perfect
harmony, each cloverleaf intersection provides
each participant with a sense of exhilaration
as the effortless starting and stopping and flow
keeps unfolding.

F. Succession of variations. Couple in
cross-hatched convertible looks at freight-train
chugging along beside them. Tarpaulin's
broken loose from its flat-car pinnings, and
flapping reveals three cross-hatched
convertibles, same year and model as theirs.

G. Car is about to pass them, couple up front,
cross-hatched convertible like theirs. They're
waving at each other, the two couples, like
long-lost friends, laughing at the false solemnity
of the three cross-hatched convertibles
chugging along beside them, wending their
way past vast factory roofs with the
brand-names slanted towards the sun, and
delicate vine tendrils moving outward from
the headlights in the car beside them, with
a moppet head with goody-goody curls
bumping in the breeze from the speed, and
the chihuahua turning sideways to stare at the
two couples disapprovingly. NO ONE in
front seat . . .

H.   *Mostly one sees produce on its way to market
       on most of the ramps and levels of the meaty
       cloverleaf intersection, and black trucks
       taking away the remnants and discards,
       heading in the opposite direction towards the
       false city half-buried in the muck of the
       ex-lagoon.*

I.   *No good to stay put in order to pick up some
       rounding the leaf pointers. The more one
       stays put, the more one is removed from the
       casual system that is working in harmony with
       itself, effortlessly, with truck drivers enjoying
       the sunlight as it warms their frizzled arm-hair
       on the side of the truck cab. Overhead, the
       dirigible, Orientals, planes in V formation,
       mail-sack dropping, circle of postmen on
       stilts, roughnecks in trees, man in tux with
       hook just under mail-sack.*

J.   *Filling station. Pretty girl gassing up smiles
       at driver of yellow school bus having oil
       checked; pickup truck suspended on metal
       pole in midair. In it, paralytic propped up
       in back, priest on ladder beside him—blessing
       —closed eyes—*

K.   *Weight of solid structures in any Holy City
       thrusts sideways and upwards. Labyrinths
       of tunnels and courtyards and metal catwalks.
       Screened residences. Behind metal fences.
       Of those who may be planning a further
       collapse in order to construct some new and
       much weightier system of Holy City*

Geography, all this bearing down on the older structures, squeezing still existent intersections on teetering traffic cubes temporarily shored up by girders which only complicate the system on the lower ramps and egresses—

L.   *Hideous stone grimaces—misconstrued—heralded as great and wondrous rounding the leaf unity.*

M.   *AUTOMBOL.*

N.   *peeing out a*

O.   *Limousine is parallel to moppet's car.*

P.   *Man in tux rises out of the flowers.*

Q.   *Realize it's a hearse.*

R.   *Rolls down window.*

S.   *I do same.*

T.   *Passes out brief-case.*

U.   *I take it.*

V.   *In front-seat, but not driving (me).*

W.   *Chihuahua in back plus moppet.*

X.   *Open brief-case.*

Y.   *My "Holy City Geography Book."*

Z.   *I open to end-papers.*

I'd been reading the steam. And at the same time I was having a fantastic "Holy City Seizure!" And with no cloud machine and no Diana Vienna!

White globs!

I yelled into the mouthpiece, "Who are you?"

More globs . . . smear chest and buttocks . . .

I found my way back to my quarters, collapsing on my Civil War hospital bed, exhausted. I stared at my "Holy City Geography Book" with loathing. Green cloth, frayed edges. Title in black block Roman. Forming a cloverleaf traffic intersection pattern, were the names of the authors:

> BISHOP T. L-W DAO
>
> REV. ANNIE MULDANE
>
> FR. SCULLER
>
> RABBI BORG

In the right-hand lower corner, I noticed a small *d*, inked into the green cloth by Diana Vienna the day she was appointed my prophecy collator. Such frayed edges! And those brown spots! The result of some particularly damp summer, long past. My fingers skirted them—fecal discharge contamination terror.

I devised a cover of my own—a Japanese cellophane sheet—coated over with a gouache of a window, with four panes, all black. Thus did I obliterate the bespotted intersection. A normal night view. Except for the flat stone glued to the center of the four panes. And except for the Walt Whitman skin-and-beard sections glued around the stone, sections pried off my W.W. replica.

The THE was in the upper left-hand pane.
The OR was in the upper right-hand pane.
The CHID was in the lower left-hand pane.
The STORIES was in the lower right-hand pane.

I fell asleep, holding the book tilted sideways in my lap.

The following day, Miss Hinckle, in her guise as non-government Environment Comptroller, checked all books and possessions, and tagged them:

ROUNDING THE LEAF!
SAFELY ON MY WAY!
ROUNDING THE LEAF!

I gave Barry Wingate my disguised "Holy City Geography Book." As Guard, he was subject to perfunctory questioning and searching. I gave Miss Hinckle the faceless W.W. replica as a going-away present. She kissed me full on the lips. Our spectacles clicked, and made a lobster-claws-grappling sound. She complimented me on my explorer doll-house, and tagged me:

ROUNDING THE LEAF!
SAFELY ON MY WAY!
ROUNDING THE LEAF!

After waiting a discreet amount of time, sure that she'd passed along the alphabet, past *W*, I hurried to Barry Wingate's quarters, on the other side of the quadrangle. He was not in his 1917 Bomb Shelter, on the top-floor of the Guard Tower. Just sandbags. And in the dust—a flat stone, the stone I'd glued to the center of the four panes, the turquoise shaped like an orchid that I'd caught, such a long time ago, falling through the sky from the "moon."

ROUNDING THE LEAF?
SAFELY ON MY WAY?
ROUNDING THE LEAF?

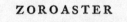

ZOROASTER

Gertrud Schmidlapp was wearing a black parka trimmed in black fox, black leather slacks, and black glacier boots. She seemed to enjoy her role of "Keeper of the Flame," mistress of a central body of psycho-dynamic knowledge that would stand us in good stead in the outside world. Dr. Schmidlapp was increasingly taken up with his researches in the inter-relationships between air, weather, family ties, dreams, and "breath pulse," and so it was up to her to transmit this body of psycho-dynamic knowledge to his patients, constantly expanding and modifying it to conform to his latest findings. Each and every one of his patients was sick and tired of low-spirited behavior patterns and personality repeats which had spread out from ads, movie-screens, photo mags, and TV hybrid entertainment surrounds into a virtual psycho-flood of fluttering mental pre-and-after images, the minuscule dots of which formed a nubile psycho-fog shaped like a tempting but amorphuous sex organ (breast, phallus, foot, mouth, etc.) that had no doubt first seduced and then dulled the perennial

"I Can Do Anything Better Than You" adolescent buried in each and every one of his patients.

Us patients, I should confess, for I'd been under light observation all summer, after a nine-month trek on the Orchard Trail, compiling panorama memories, followed by a nine-month trek from metropolis to metropolis—more about that later. Hiatus!

MY FAVORITE PANORAMA MEMORY

four women on a porch
cross out words in a
long novel about three
generations (skirt-
sleeves to shirt-
sleeves), one word
at a time, slowly,
one word per woman,
handing the book
around, each with a
red crayon, and every
so often, a page is
turned, another two
pages done, chapter
finished, Part One
—THE BEGINNING—
finished, about the
foundry in the small
village, and I look
to see how far along
they are, hours to
go yet, hours. Drowsiness
assails me, a
hummy feeling all

through my body, the
way certain grass
fields tickle. I
want them so much
to sip cokes, raising
the bottles at
different times slowly,
but they don't.
If only they'd put
the novel down, and
do their nails, buffing
it's called, isn't
it? Then they could
take down their hair,
and unplait the parts
of it that hang down
to their waists, and
do it up again, for
now it's dusk and
time to go to bed.

PHONE RINGS. ELBERTA ANSWERS. I GO IN: MUMMERS.
MUMMY HAS DIED OF CANCER-OF-THE-MOUTH, WHICH
MUMMERS BLAMES ON FOUL SILENT TREATMENTS PLUS
LEAVING HATE NOTES ON THE STAIRS PLUS TAKING OFF
ON MYSTERY JAUNTS. LAST HATE NOTE: "NURSE-
SABOTEUSE WON'T HOLD MY APPETITE INDUCER UP TO
MY LIPS FOR EVEN ONE PUFF, OR UP TO MY NOSE FOR
EVEN ONE SNIFF, OR INTO MY—" KENTUCKY BURIAL,
BEHIND THE PEOPLED LIFE RAFT. OBELISK DRAPED WITH
FLAG. I PEEKED UNDER IT: NO NAME! GRAFFITI
SPRAYED ON, THAT'S ALL—"PHIL"—CONTINUE TREK—
ARRIVE AT NIGHT, MOON.

There I am on the porch,
swinging in the icy air,
listening for the four
doors to shut softly.
Their radios come on,
little swing tunes, as
clouds pass over the
moon, casting shadows
on the black overpasses
on the outskirts of the
apple orchards. I peer
in each room, in turn,
through the transom,
and watch each one's
scissors snipping away
at the Icebox Orchid
design. When the lacy
flower is cut out, each
one sets it on fire with
a long wooden match
struck against their
sturdy shoes. The radios
are silent now, and the
orange glow in the four
transoms fades. In the
morning, I will collect
the ashes. Absolute
happiness.

My suite was fitted out with a maze of motion reflectors, nighttime seeing eyes, machines that stored and correlated sleep movements, shifts in metabolism, characteristic gestures, effluvia, and most important: "breath pulse." Until I could figure out how to continue safely on my way,

rounding the leaf, safely on my way, in my new circum-
stances, it seemed a solution of sorts to remain in Dr.
Schmidlapp's care—at least for a year or so. My new
circumstances?

I was traveling through Grapefruit Country when I
happened on a public library attached to a one-room
agriculture school. I spent the day in the reading room,
leafing through old copies of *Citrus*, when I happened on a
photo of an orchid, a "mascot," flourishing in a Texas
grove—red leaf under two close rows of fleshy protuber-
ances that erupted into three flowers with red dahlia-like
spikes circling the tubular center, plus four curled long
leaves spreading out on each side of the main red leaf. I
tore it out, and mailed it to Mummers, home in Hode:
Monday. On Friday, he was planning to leave for a sojourn
at Dr. Schmidlapp's new research center in Iceland, as he
was having trouble "breeding"—so it sounded over the
phone. He died on a Thursday, in his sleep. Obelisk,
Kentucky. Mummers never received my "cutting"—it ar-
rived, its envelope a jumble of postmarks, two days after
the ceremony, having been sent from Hobe, Florida, to
Johe, Arizona, and from there to Jole, Georgia. By mis-
take, I'd spelled "Hode" "Home," with a *J*-like *H*. How it
reached Hode, I'll never know. I took the unopened en-
velope to the attic, at *Locust*, where I'd left the "Native
Innards" box at the time of Mummy-Phil's demise, along
with the explorers' doll-house. Balanced on the envelope
were jagged fragments of the "Icebox" lightbulb, which
I'd found in a black sachet bag dangling in Mummers'
bedroom at Hode. I placed these additions inside the Lucky
Strike carton, beside the "Debs" orchid, the "Edith's
Death" orchid, etc.—a collection that would legally belong
to me, if, and it was a big if, the family affairs ever became
disentangled. Mummy-Phil's consortium's assets (into

which Mummers had funneled his resources) were frozen (Lawyer ※1), impounded in various fake countries (Lawyer ※2), nonexistent except "on paper" (Lawyer ※3)— and so I could count on a meagre income, enough to make ends meet—providing I lived in a shack in some winterless rural area, and providing I grew my own food. And so, I went job-hunting for a position with a government conglomerate in some major metropolis.

Months passed!

Routine: I'd arrive by bus, check in at a businessman's hotel, then go for a walk in the morning, through deserted streets, (5 A.M.), till I found (6 A.M.) a movie palace. I'd go next door to an all-nite diner, and order a huge breakfast—waffles, hash browns, scrambled eggs, cereal, tomato juice; I'd eat it slowly (in the above order, saving coffee for last) and watch the workmen and domestics shovel in their coffee-ands, eyeing me suspiciously (8 A.M.)—they'd meander off to work, grumpily. I'd hang around the boxoffice till the cashier opened it up, and then I'd buy a ticket for an earlybird movie and big band stageshow—so as to feel tiptop for my job interview lunch. It gave me a big boot to sit in an eerily lit movie palace at nine in the morning, with a handful of stray oddballs who obviously had no place else to go—old ladies with string bags bulging with salvaged newspapers and foraged food, wall-eyed galoots from the mountains, zonked runaways with cigarette burns on their arms and scabs on their knuckles— sipping cough medicine out of throat-shaped blue bottles, and—mustn't forget *them*—zombie girls from suburban bungalows—with a certain stiff way of walking down the aisle, as if they were sore from incredible sexual excesses indulged in the night before—or, more likely—as if they

were guarding against some big city assault by trying to
appear as wooden, in an amputated way, as possible. What
a relief to see the lights dim, and to look up and see a night
sky revolving on the ceiling, with all the astrological signs
of the zodiac outlined in twinkling stars, and with luminous
white clouds that gracefully formed and as gracefully
vanished, part of some slow-motion cosmic steeplechase.

The newsreel cocoanuts always jolted me (I instinctively
covered my hair), plopping down on the beach as the
hurricane of current events gathered force, and often I'd
scurry up the aisle and down into the men's room, where,
in a cubicle, I'd wait out a wheezing fit, and then return,
perhaps having missed the short subjects and previews of
coming attractions—at which point (9:30 A.M.) the cur-
tains would close and the lights would come on, inducing
momentary terror in me, terror that some time woof had
made me miss the movie (another trip up aisle)—but
after a respectful pause, the lights would dim, the curtains
would open, and the feature would start.

THE END! All wobbly-looking because of the closing
curtains! Yanked out of my trance, I'd rush to the first
row, and crane around to see if perhaps a few three-
square-meals-a-day-steady-job types had infiltrated among
us early birds. And, finally, after the organist had com-
pleted his medley, the lights would dim, and the
curtains part to reveal a big band rising up on its platform,
out of the pit, blaring forth a rowdy medley of Fleet's -
In - Saturday - Nite - Honkytonk - Slap - Those - Thighs -
Keep - Your - Money - In - Your - Jockstrap Polkas. I'd
scrutinize each musician's face as he soloed, transported by
each improvisation, and after the big band had sunk back
down, I'd sit for a moment, charged with energy, breath-
ing deeply, full of confidence in my ability to make my
mark in the world—rounding the leaf! Safely on my way!

Hah!

Exhaust, from one bus. Exhaustion!

Clammy hands, vertigo—fear of falling under a careening taxi—gasp—or some gov't limousine with flashing lights—pant pant—sirens—amplified voices—the astonishing midday pace of pedestrians and autos—struggle for breath (drowning sensation)—brain throbs—sickly smell of the air above subway gratings, like the vomit of mutants who've gorged on synthetic electricity. Lugging each leaden foot, drained of energy, I'd stagger blindly towards my hotel. So much glittery stuff on the sidewalks, mica, pavement-and-crack, pavement-and-crack, all tilted, and with horrible blasts of crowd sounds, yells of rage, hatred shrieks! Whispered questions. Lost! Incomprehensible directions drowned out by the roar of dynamos blocks away, back at the movie palace (12 A.M.)—newsreel cocoanuts (men's room)—different feature, and the inverted bowl above me is an ocean with fish and nymphs and gods—audience looks the same—place woof panic—rush out to travel agency next door, must book departure. If only my wallet and identification weren't back at the hotel, ask the attractive employee about inoculation requirements for Brazil—writing my question down, pretending I'm "mute"—and writing down a P.S.—where is such-and-such a hotel—through that glass door, sir—she's pointing—the agency adjoins my hotel lobby, it seems—I rush through the lobby, collapse on the jump seat in the elevator, fight my way to my suite through air that resists me like jelly full of microbes. Gasping, staring periodically at the radium dial of my watch resting on its pillow beside mine, I set a deadline (4 P.M.) to make the phone call to the company official regarding our job interview lunch—phone rings! (3:45).

". . . no idea it was so late, appetite has gone up the

spout, er, microbes must have sneaked into the sanitized glass . . ."

"Just who is this?"

"Next week, if I'm still in town, hah hah hah, I'll do my death, er, rattle imitation for you. Just joking. Actually, next week, I'll be—haven't worked out my itinerary exactly—"

"Just who is this?"

". . . argh . . .".

Being a patient agreed with me, as did Iceland. After a few months, I was in touch with my breath pulse, and my struggles to control the involuntary panting that began with Mummers' decease were largely successful. My outlook perked up dramatically.

One day, a written message from Dr. Schmidlapp brightened my breath pulse tempo:

> *Going to the movies makes you feel*
> *schizophrenic. Each time you go, it*
> *seems as if no time has passed since*
> *your last movie. There's a person*
> *(You ✳1) who only lives in movie palaces,*
> *and there's someone else who*
> *lives in inferior places: childhood*
> *bedroom, distant attic, ragweed gullies,*
> *store windows chockful of pink trusses,*
> *this very compound known as the Schmidlapp*
> *Compound. You (✳2)—scary. And yet*
> *beautiful. But if I were you ✳1 and*
> *✳2, I'd concentrate on creating a you ✳3,*
> *a composite of you ✳1 and you ✳2.*
> *A referee. Only you can do it. If I*

try to do it for you, Me ☿870421 *would*
come into being, in you. No. Bring
you ☿3 *into being, and you'll be way*
ahead of the game.

Reykjavík, a few miles south, was a pleasant city,
population 75,000, with air purer than any other city of
comparable size, which undoubtedly influenced Dr.
Schmidlapp's shift of locale from White Island. As I soon
learned from Gertrud, Reykjavík was known as The
Smokeless City—there was no coal smoke whatsoever, as
its houses were heated with hot water from hot springs,
the geysers of which splattered and darkened the black
boulder steppes that stretched in between the glaciers,
forming a pleasing snag-toothed zigzag pattern of black
vs. white. Mrs. Schmidlapp (Gertrud) followed the prec-
edent of the first Mrs. Schmidlapp (Helga) and had
constructed a star-shaped cluster of permanent green-
houses. Soon after her marriage to the doctor, she began
building up a collection of orchids, orchids which thrived
on the sphagnum she found near the hot springs, hot
springs which also provided her with an economical source
of heat. Plus which there were few dangerous insects—no
ants, no cockroaches, no mosquitoes of the anopheles spe-
cies, and very few flies. Helga lived outside the Schmidlapp
Compound, in a comfortable cottage a few hundred yards
down the hill, out of earshot of the yelpy police dogs
that patrolled the circumference of the compound. Ger-
trud and Helga were on the best of terms, and the three
of us, when the weather was sunny, sometimes went on
sphagnum gathering expeditions. We'd stop off on our
way back to window-shop in Reykjavík. Sometimes, we'd
sit at a bar and drink cocktails, and tell off-color jokes.
Helga's favorite was:

*What did Connie Boswell, the famous singer, ask the
famous explorer, Osa Johnson?*

*Fill in local color, something about Africa, personal
anecdote if you've traveled there—stomach troubles,
best safari, high-rise architecture in the cities,
bargains, good business opportunities, insect life.*

*What do you think of women who allow strangers to see
their pubic hair?*

*The same as men who mince bare-arsed. You don't expect
a man to mince bare-arsed well, and to be able to mince
period is remarkable, replies Osa Johnson.*

Helga had sold her portable greenhouse in Norway—
for scrap. She had no special hobbies now. She was con-
tent to get through the day.

Gertrud sometimes confided in me. She was worried
about Helga. Her breath pulse was erratic.

All that summer in Iceland, I was plagued by grandiose
fantasies of industrial sabotage. I had intense "boy in-
ventor" longings to start up a small firm that would
mushroom into a gigantic conglomerate, wooed by re-
gimes the world over. Country A, say, hires it—Country
B is target. Expensive cuts of meat restricted to govern-
ment B bigwigs turn to licorice-flavored wads at official
functions, with networks of blue veins in which parades
of white lumps crawl along onto dignitaries' plates, talking
cockroaches with minute transistors attached, spreading
meaningless catch phrases:

PROFITS MEAN FINE ABACUS

MEDLEY UNBALANCED

BANANA BLONDE

WHAT DID ANDY WEAR? ANDY WORE—

A big boom shattered the silence. A ball of fire rolled across the glacier.

"The spectacle of mankind's inventions through the ages—"

Mrs. Schmidlapp had to cup her hands around her mouth and yell.

"The spectacle of mankind's inventions through the ages—"

Huddling together, we regrouped in the pit in the hut. Dominant words in the conversation were:

INVENTIONS

OLDER

CHINA

DISEASES

WISDOM

The patients consisted of (excluding me):

Gladys Jacomb . . . . COCKNEY EX-VAUDEVILLIAN
Dennis Jacomb . . . . HER HUSBAND, RETIRED STEVEDORE
Evalyn B—— . . . . HAIR DESIGNER
Georgia B—— . . . . CHAIR SHINER
Patti B——— . . . . SHARE COMBINER
Terri B—— . . . . GLARE DIVINER
Zitti B——— . . . . SPARE LINER
Herman Ott . . . . AUTOMOBILE SALESMAN
Helga . . . . EX-MRS. SCHMIDLAPP (BEER SMELL)

Which one of these people used the dominant words first?

MRS. SCHMIDLAPP

"You were saying—the spectacle of mankind's inventions—"

"Yes, yes. What if mankind has no health or ability? Certain ones—Zoroasters—will emerge: inventors. Using these inventions will keep mankind busy, and give him ample time to lament his personal atrophy. These laments can be fed into the inventions, and subsequently, bought, traded, sold, stored, stolen, or even distributed to the recalcitrant, by force if need be."

"That's all very well, but what if, hidden in small echo units of their own devising, pockets of renegade individuals in caves, in distant uplands, subsisting on cacti liquids, jimsonweeds, bird droppings, moss in underground streams—"

Mrs. Schmidlapp interrupted me excitedly.

"Sweet renegade, it's still early in history. Man has yet to fully discover his limitations by making use of laments. Then he'll find out how to look more young, strong, and handsome as he grows older and weaker, and this is my main point: as if he were following a law of nature. Man still has plenty of time to learn how to manipulate such inventions as huge artificial limbs, for instance—big brawny affairs, the more the better. Like those oriental idols. One foot is holding a sacred lotus orchid, another foot is picking a sacred lotus blossom off a tree on a windy cranny, within view of those renegade individuals, those echo units of yours who are thereby instantly won over, another foot is holding an ancient holy text with a picture on its cover of an oriental idol, with one foot holding a sacred lotus orchid, and another foot picking a sacred lotus orchid blossom off a tree on a windy cranny, within view of those renegade individuals, those echo units of yours—"

The storm hit. Mrs. Schmidlapp rushed up the spiral staircase; golfball-size hailstones collected in patches that congealed on the plastic ceiling, and through the bubble windows, one could see the leaves being stripped from the trees, and the vines chewed to shreds.

That night, there was a charade party to cheer up Mrs. Schmidlapp. The storm had shattered many of the panes of her greenhouse, and the icy water dripping down onto the orchids had caused untold damage. Dr. Schmidlapp put in an appearance, and he was at his best. He chatted about the events of the day, tactfully avoiding the subject of the storm, and his charm, wit, and pungent comments held the floor, and all us patients (and Mrs. Schmidlapp too) were gay with laughter.

Evalyn peeled something oblong. She handed it to Georgia, who lifted up Patti's skirt, as if to straighten it. Next, Patti inspected Terri's pink bloomers, clinically, as if she saw a spot. Terri brushed Patti's hand away: bothersome bug. Zitti ate the object with prissy gestures, tossing the remnant away with ill-concealed disgust. She dismissed the others, who, bowing and scraping, moved backwards. One by one, they slipped, fell, tumbled over backwards. Zitti reached inside the folds of her blouse, and tossed the others some square bronze coins with holes in them. The others scrambled about the floor, retrieving the coins.

"BANANA!" I yelled.
"BONANZA!" Mrs. Schmidlapp shouted.

Zitti dropped the square coins in Mrs. Schmidlapp's lap, exclaiming, "With these ancient Chinese coins, you can buy many new windows, many new blooms."

The others converged on me, yanked at my hair, pummeled me, pinched me. All because I'd given the wrong answer! Regrettable incident. They were the only people in all Iceland who made me feel like an expatriate.

Soon the summer'd be over. I lay in my suite, on the floor, on a white bearskin rug, my radium watch dial on the center of its huge black tongue. I was lost in an industrial sabotage daydream. Dr. Schmidlapp enjoyed them, and encouraged me to talk them out loud when by myself—that way, the machines could correlate my tone of voice, gestures, vocabulary, facial expressions, and breath pulse.

"Feel like a re-beginning. Case 31. Two hotels. The Royale has slipped, while the New Splendid has benefited from alert management. The Debutante Grand Ball has switched for the first time to the New Splendid. The young ladies form a grand rose, as appropriate scent is released from nozzles in the air-conditioning vents. The Mayor strides towards the winner. General Pershing outfit. Puttees, mustache, baton. Tradition: General Pershing was judge of first Debutante Grand Ball—new class of moneyed people, war profits, old money people won't let them in—girls are nice-looking, tidier than old money girls, care more about appearance, making good impression, catch husband with company that might merge with Dad's company, and Mom's company. Old waiter with rouged face lunges in front of Mayor, sinks to parquet shouting: YOU'RE AWFUL! He seizes the Mayor's baton, screams, BEWARE OF THE VULTURES! He bites on the baton, as if it's an ear of corn. His mouth froths, eyes roll. Driblets of foam on parquet. A girl shouts, HE MEANS WE'RE OFFAL, OFFAL! DON'T YOU UNDERSTAND, SHIT! SHIT! SHIT! Bird screeches resound through the public address system. A black feather falls through the air, and hangs suspended, above the Mayor."

Dr. Schmidlapp entered my suite.

"I think you don't understand China yet. But what relation has China to the Buddha? None, now. China is full of diseases because it has denied the law of creation since history began—the Law of Tong: Abandon Nature. This irrevocable law will one day numb China, like some wind of black death gas that expands in a two-four-sixteen progression, changing day to night. Diseases will spread until inventions break down, untended and disused. Then some incredible renegade, hidden in a small echo unit of his own devising, will lead mankind, like a Zoroaster, back to health, wealth, and wisdom."

Dr. Schmidlapp took an orchid out of his buttonhole, and held it out to me. It had purplish leaves, an inner opening, black streaked with green, like the markings on a wasp, surrounded by a pumpkin-yellow band, bumpy and sticky. I recognized it at once as a "Native Innards."

"A lad, a flashy lad," Dr. Schmidlapp continued, "could, by breathing in the quiet of his suite, become so potent all the inventions would become mere toys, humming placidly before they run down. And someone else, a girl, a young girl of indeterminate origin, could walk, then crawl, growing weaker and weaker. Her beauty would be calculated to have the maximum effect on the impartial observer. Half her face, sinking down the side of a French window— tremendous explosion! Big ball of fire rolling where you want it to. The citizens in their coma won't hear it, though, preoccupied as they are with their own atrophy. One day, thanks to this lad and this girl, they'll return to their nebulous state, and wander through the sky, rid of inventions, China, wisdom, wealth, and older diseases, free at last of the law of creation: Abandon Nature."

Smiling at me, he put the orchid in my buttonhole, took hold of my shoulders firmly, and, like a French general, kissed me on both cheeks.

He closed the door behind him, quietly.

A few moments later, the hum of machines in the room stopped.

It seemed a reasonable assumption that I was well.

WAKING UP

Waking up surrounded by Swiss jaggedness, in the role of thorazine pianist at the Mojesta Beauty Cosmos, I thought I heard a tune coming out of the vast honeycomb of black entrances the darkness was made up of, a tune that (grrr) grew fainter the harder I strained to hear it. By deliberately falling asleep again, judging from previous experience, I knew I could sneak up on the tune, and hear enough of it to use it as my next prophecy source for the day, a discovery I'd made surrounded by Swiss jaggedness.

Say the half-heard tune went from C to A to D to C, cup-shaped, with a bum-tiddy-bum-bum-bum in the background, vaguely martial, but with an ingratiating yuck-yuck calypso beat struggling through the spit-and-polish, waking up surrounded by Swiss jaggedness, I'd think, like as not, I was waking up surrounded by:

AFRICAN AFTERNOON

Brass band of black postmen playing for
British officers. Polo teams line up.
Mallets whirl through air: invisible circles.
Homage to Princess. All together now: BIG
ROAR OF WELCOME. Gaga jaw, froth.
Gov-Gen yells HORSE BLANKET. BIGGER
ROAR OF WELCOME. Froth, peke licks it.
Gaga jaw. "She's a jolly good fellow . . ."
Grabs blanket, throws it over her. Jiggling
blanket. Natives flee—curse of the—

Along with the scene, certain hints (next move indi-
cator) and certainties (prophecy) would cluster around
each tune, issuing forth out of the honeycomb of entrances
the darkness seemed made up of. Example.

HINTS

1. Great orderly thought cubes.

2. Life The Big Squasher.

3. The two docks . . .

CERTAINTIES

1. Don't go near cities to South. Violence.

2. Stay put.

3. "The longer youth one has, one is as a rule
more long-lived."
        —Olav Swartz

Waking up that winter, in the role of thorazine pianist, with a view of Mont Blanc outside my one-chair balcony, a fine tune came out of the black entrances: la la la, oompah, pah, oompah, tring! Tsiganesque. A patriotic air—Albanian perhaps—a touch of Transylvania—flute trills, pizzicato, cadenzas—sissy embellishments—another whole scene!

> *Carousing detective . . . yanks open a*
> *door . . . bloody geezer falls out . . . in*
> *the basement . . . watching a movie . . .*
> *the children in the wooden freezer—*

Certain hints and clusters of certainties moved into the scene:

HINTS

1.   Great orderly thought cubes.

2.   Life The Big Squasher.

3.   The two docks . . .

CERTAINTIES

1.   Be on the look out for a winding corridor
with windows looking out on a quadrangle,
a corridor with amusing little steps up and
little steps down—reminiscent of Japanese
bridges on cheap crockery—steps come at
irregular intervals, slowing one down just
as one gets going at a nice clip—cosy
resting places sprinkled about with three
mirrors set into the wall so one's reflection—

2. *Someone on the opposite side of the quadrangle is racing down an identical corridor from window to window, staring at me, hurrying on, staring at me, trying to force the window open (no time!) to tell me something that will irrevocably set the course—*

3. *Nobody around, except this visitor-stranger rapping on the window, trying to force it open, just as I am trying to force my—*

A feeling of immense power surged through me, as if outward moving weather map arrows were under my control, and were speeding from the Arctic Circle in all directions, gathering momentum, darkening skies above valleys and mountains into a huge black bruise. Ach, the bigger the surge, the fainter the tune, the bigger the mystery, the sadder the letdown.

Waking up, surrounded by Swiss jaggedness, I couldn't shake myself loose from the following semi-remembrance:

THE TWO DOCKS

Looking down on two docks. Glimpsed from a seedy waterfront hotel room with blinking sign that lights up harbor at precise intervals—vista, blackout, vista. Dearth of any liner in between docks forces me to savor air where it might have been anchored. Air turns baboon's rear-end shade of purple, commoner color in seaports than you'd think. Forces me to savor air where liner might have been, with its lights a-glimmer in the dawn, a few roistering passengers in evening togs

dancing under the fading stars . . . and beneath
them, sullen sailors stare out of portholes dully,
their eyes filmed over, as if blind or playing
music. Pshaw. They are not blind. They are
only thinking of certain figures of shore-leave
desire: dance-hall dames in silk evening dresses
with damp spots from sweat from dancing so
hard. Good-hearted girls, just about ready for
bed, if it weren't for those wealthy executives
in black limousines, fingering plastic orchids in
silver vases bolted to the niches between rear-view
window and back-seat side windows, orchids lit
by blue courtesy lights above ebony scalloped
ashtrays, and now—the sailors reeling along the
sidewalk in twos and threes wink knowingly at
each other as the executives rap on the side
windows of their limousines with big heavy
potentate rings. The sailors leap in, the doors
close quietly, they sit on jump seats, hunched
up, resting their elbows on the soft angora sox
of the executives, whose big legs straddle the
jump seats, ah, the luxurious penthouse is five
minutes away on a hilltop overlooking the two
docks—whiskey, cards, a private jazz band, a
party! Lively people enter, soccer players, amused
to find each other breaking training, glider
pilots, ski enthusiasts, young boxers, expert divers,
gleaming from oils, the lights turn low, they
stretch out helter-skelter on soft carpeting, soft
sighs of pleasure arise in the darkness, sucky
sounds, grunts, the farty sounds of wet bodies
coming apart, and now the dance-hall dames
enter, the executives are nude on the sofas,
balloons are popping, on the floor writhing
bodies—

Actually, I'd arrived from Iceland (Genoa) via freighter, and debarked so late at night, I hit the hay immediately. The blinking sign woke me up at dawn. Propped up on my elbow, I raised the shade: the two docks were empty.

Waking up that morning, surrounded by Swiss jaggedness, in the role of thorazine pianist named Zoroaster, I got past THE TWO DOCKS by managing to doze off again. I sneaked up on a tune, a jaunty marimba two-step—zing zing bonk—zing zing ba-ta-ta-bzzzzzzz—

BLONDE COMPOUND

Inter-connected patios in Blonde Compound, husbands and wives go different ways, meet as sun sinks, small-talk of flower arrangements in picture windows, the day's defectors—more and more and more the bright people are opting for an isolated way of life where social contact is held to a minimum—

Certain hints and certainties moved into the scene:

HINTS

1. *Morning air breathes on elbow, awakening you as gently as angora cat.*

2. *Loving pet breathes on elbow of its slave in holy zoo where all animals are gods.*

3. *Pets—fantastic actors. If you let them, they'll re-enact puppy-dog, kitty-cat, bunny-rabbit days of yore.*

4. *Try to describe road sign to pet: regard
this as serious assignment. It's raining, and
the drops drip down the sign's surface
like transparent bugs in sportive chase,
enlarging the printed matter on the sign
as they race about. Next, wait for shutter to
close in pet's eyes. Look into its eyes. When
they glow like glass road markers caught
in a headlight, peer into them.*

CERTAINTIES

1. *New expanse of Happy New Year Times
awaits you.*

2. *Urgent: find signposts . . . basement . . .
Gertrud . . . cloverleaf intersection . . . vast
factory roofs . . . chihuahua . . . great
thought cubes . . .*

I opened my eyes. I was sitting in a chair in
my pajamas. I'd sleep-walked! The bloody geezer . . . the
two docks . . . the Blonde Compound . . . Happy New
Year Times . . . their reverberations faded. As usual, while
not quite awake, I felt the presence of the orchid attic
overhead, above the chair I'd sleep-walked to. I tended
to look at walls and ceilings as concealants at the Mojesta
Beauty Cosmos, wishfully thinking the orchid attic in
Hode was in whatever part of the building I hadn't seen,
rather than out of reach, on another continent. On this
particular morning, transfixed against the afterglow sil-

houette of a luxuriant "psychological bride" dream, I envisioned the familiar attic stairs, skeletal, with bashed-in places from heavy furniture and steamer trunks, the white pine roof with bits of fuzz caught in the spider webs that always moved as one walked past them, setting gray flecks in motion, flecks like down from the legs of tiny birds. Placed under the eye-shaped window, past the ebony spittoon, the box—if only I could ease my memory of the attic past the kicking line of "Dog Roots" Girls—

Waking up that winter morning, expanding vibration circles in assorted colors widened in a steady even flow, on the underside of my eyelid, making it impossible to inch onto the box. The vibration circles kept streaming outward mercilessly, and when I stared at my thumb, thinking this would interrupt the flow, the circles thereupon constricted themselves on my thumb-nail with such intensity, it was as if an entire Aurora Borealis was squeezed under a transparent thimble. In a desperate attempt to disperse the vibration circles, I put my thumb in my mouth, and pressed the nail against the roof of my mouth, hard. Great lungings and wheelings welled up, happy throbbings, echoed grunts of pleasure that quickened and connected, turning into a scream that seemed to come from someone else, a scream that kept replenishing itself effortlessly, so effortlessly, why, it was like sitting in a tepid bath, watching the water redden and darken, only to realize peeing out pleasantly is a never-ending supply of one's own lifeblood.

A new tune fragment. One note: duh-duh-duh-duh-duh-duh-duh. The results?

EMOTIONAL JURISDICTION

Cackling ghosts line up. Gaga froth.

HINTS

None.

CERTAINTIES

None.

HYBRID HINT-CERTAINTY-SCENE

Seeming eternity.
Clickety-clacking up steep roller-coaster track,
baffled by overhead warnings in hieroglyphics
(distant hoots of pleasure)—how delightful to
emerge into the blinding air, hurtling towards
the ocean, careening through the sky, catapulting
around so fast

GAP

*   one's own scream seems to come*
from someone else, a scream that keeps
replenishing itself so effortlessly, it's like sitting
in a tepid bath, watching the water redden and
darken, only to realize one is peeing out a
never-ending supply of one's own lifeblood.

There was nothing to do but give up trying to ease my attic memory past the spittoon, as, at this point, my "psychological bride" dream swerved to the fore. I saw the faint afterglow of the balls of a Dalmatian, moving like slow-motion yo-yos, alternately, each ball a perfect little Rubens breast with mottled pink and black skin, nippleless, true, but so cunningly dependent looking, they

seemed to smell of vanilla in a Dutch cubbyhole of a
room, with snow falling outside, and silent people gliding
over frozen-over dikes, visiting their beloveds, circuitously
progressing from town to town, each participant exhil-
arated by the stopping and starting, the succession of
variations leading back to regularized repetitions—a prog-
ress in harmony with the languorous up-down yo-yo mo-
tion of the Rubens breast dog balls, alternating ceaselessly,
the motion of which formed two straight lines, lines that
dovetailed with two cracks in the ceiling, cracks that
promised a gateway (illusory) to the orchid attic in the
empty house on another continent.

At which point, fully wakeful, I absorbed the actual
room I was in—chair on which I was sitting, silver lim-
ousine vase bolted to the wall under a snapshot of whoever
was dominant in the room at the time (me), and in the
vase, an innocuous light violet orchid, with five spikes
growing out of its pink stem, full of crested fluted yellow
specks on a velvety background of arching petals, curved
like seven tongues fanning out of a hollering mouth:
LOVE O' TOMORROW—discovered in Panama by Olav Swartz,
Swedish professor of botany, born in 1769, lived with a
succession of foster parents, married one of his students
(1816), fathered child (1817), and died the following
year, too soon to see his discovery bloom for the second
time (eighteen-year cycle). This orchid had arrived on my
birthday several weeks before, with a card enclosed:

> FROM MY SUNSHINE TEXAS GREENHOUSE
> COME STAY   BARRY

Sitting up in the rumpled bed, surrounded by Swiss
jaggedness, rubbing her eyes, was Ypra, thorazine mezzo.

She whispered something in German to Sarge, thorazine tenor. Happily, I sang out, "La la la, oompah, oompah tring! Ba-ta-ta bzzzzzzz, zing zing zing!"

I scrambled into my sex costume (zouave pants with sewn-up fly, dagger, no shirt, kepi at rakish angle, white calf-skin boots, kohl around eyes, silk panties worn as kerchief around neck) and climbed back into bed . . . Monday, Tuesday, Wednesday, Thursday, Friday, Saturday, Sunday, Monday, Tuesday, Winter, Summer, Autumn, Spring, sickness, health, forever and forever—

> *Ypra watches Sarge, me. Sings to me, love songs
> from his homeland, about picnics in mountains
> with his girl, Ypra, graduation day, triplets in his
> arms. "Lick them clean." I refuse. Ypra, me.
> Half-puma. Escape to forests. Sarge follows.
> Blizzard. We hibernate.*

A midget arm, muscular in its way, groped the air, reaching for the knob set in the head of the bedstead. "ARMADA . . . TIRANA . . . FRONTIERS CLOSED . . . DIRIG—"

I reached over and clicked it off.

I emptied the bottle of its final three capsules, stolen blue Beauty Casino capsules for clients only: not for the likes of us.

FAUTEUIL

In such a situation, one is afraid to face the endlessness of it, no? An endlessness which seems to have arbitrarily imposed itself on one by a fluke. If only one had been born Swiss, the daughter of a well-to-do grocer. One could expand the fine foods department, correspond with growers all over the world, searching out an out-of-the-ordinary olive, a cheese from a high altitude in the Andes, dried foodstuff from a remote oasis in the Gobi—hein? Hein? No. One is nineteen, handsome, blond, with a new mustache that keeps one awake at night; it makes scratching noises as one tosses about in bed, burying one's face in one's hot pillow to blot out the flickers of sick yellow light that disturb one's rest. Distant gunfire. Everybody up! Time for machine-gun practice. Everybody up! Time to ram the dummy stuffed with sawdust in the guts with one's bayonet. YPRA the cadets call it—YPRA, a popular name across the border, for farm girls, small-town stenographers, café hostesses, telephone switchboard operators, and barmaids. Everybody up! Time to press down on the TNT charge with both hands, very hard (HARDER

the Sarge yells)—it's only a rehearsal, why try? The side-
walk running beside the river, the gentle Meuse, what's
happened to it? Suddenly fragmented, everyone is looking
at one in astonishment. The lady in the lavender lace dress
with the parasol standing under the acacia tree, the one
selling raffle tickets on a scrawny chicken for the war
effort, is in pink burnt underwear now, no, it's a corset
with holes in it, as if many men had singed her with
huge cigars, hein?—and she's quite, quite bald—no, there
it is, her hair, swinging on a tree branch—perhaps one
should shinny up the by now leafless tree to rescue it
before she notices her predicament—no, the Commandant
is leaning out the Schloss window; he looks apoplectic!
The Sarge will explain everything, that is if he doesn't
try to save his own skin. ENEMY ADVANCING the
Commandant yells, slamming the shutters so hard, one
swings open again, and dangles lopsidedly. He has shat-
tered its upper hinge in his rage. Senseless to tell him
what caused the little explosion—soon no one will care
about the little accident.

In such a situation, even funeral parlor work will not
defer one, except from the front lines, the trenches, dog-
fights in the sky, and inching along (poor devils) in a
submarine past an uncoiling series of observation towers
that follow the contours of the seventy-mile canal that
winds through sandstorm gorges to the ocean, and free-
dom! Twenty feet per diem, allowing time to siphon in
sufficient algae to replenish energy nonexistent staples
(ah, for a pinch of flour) once provided . . . just like
one, to fret about such "slownesses," when the immediate
problem is—how to escape being in the surface corps,
those bunches of men who move around pleasure parks,
forming squares, oblongs, circles—with dispatch. The

Sarge. He's so gruff, half-Arab, half-Greek, he doesn't
belong in this country in the first place. Half-scarab, half-
geek, he's a small-time smuggler who slithered his way
out of jail by inventing "military exploits" (slipping ground
glass in enemy food at diplomatic functions across the
border)—always sharpens his pocketknife, spits wine at
doddering ladies of the evening as they pass beneath the
barracks windows, knitting as they amble along—now
it's Saturday night, and the enemy guns are silent. Feign-
ing drunkenness, one plops on his bunk, "passes out,"
one's hand inches under the covers, as one snores vocif-
erously: contact is made—chest-hair stiff as copper wire,
and, instead of outrage, he guides one's hand further, to
more copper wire, reaches for one's other hand—a hard
wet kiss on one cheek, then the other, as if he's proudly
bestowing a medal—a grunt of satisfaction—BE CAREFUL,
THEY'LL HEAR US—CALL ME YPRA—YOU SAY I AM A LEPER
AGAIN I KILL YOU—YPRA, YPRA—THAT'S BETTER, DON'T YOU
WORRY, YOU YOUNG ONES, AH, YOU CAN'T HURT ME, I AM
TOUGH!—SHIT RAZOR-BLADES WITHOUT A PEEP, SO TOUGH—
MY GIRL VIENNA HAS GIVEN ME A DISEASE, UNDERSTAND?
—CALL ME YPRA—I JUST DID—AGAIN—YPRA, YPRA, YPRA
—NOW ARE YOU SATISFIED?—YOU CALL ME LEPER AFTER
I GIVE MYSELF TO YOU?—tears, recriminations, one prom-
ises to be faithful, to exchange love-blood—out with his
knife—he aims at one's chest—wouldn't the arm do?—
no, it is the custom among his people—the siren! It is
dawn, time for machine-gun practice, and after that, while
the others are at prayer, one can see, with a spyglass stolen
from the militia's stores, the food piled high behind the
plate-glass window of the Swiss grocery store across the
border, not ten yards beyond the sentry pacing back and
forth across the zebra-striped pavement. One can see the
pretty girl (Ypra?) in the white smock and apron placing

a chocolate cake in the center of the window (must be seven, one can set one's watch by her-and-cake) next to a ham, above a plate of star-shaped cookies, above a bowl of brown eggs, in the place of honor: the center.

In such a situation, one wishes: if only I'd been born Swiss, financially independent due to the foresight of frugal ancestors who kept within severe budgets in order to live on the interest of the interest of their investments in mildly war-torn areas, on my way to a lecture on THE GREEK MYTHS REFRACTED IN MURCAN PAYMENTS—that is "pavements" as the young folks say in the Middle "Sud" of "Murca"—they are lazy-lipped and adorable!—on my way, in my sleigh, in the hazy crazy moonlight! SHMALL TOWN PAYMENT *vs.* SCHMALL TOWN PAVEMENT. It is not dumb to be lazy-lipped. Whole new musics of the surl—sons of the surl! It is bedder zounting zan SOY-YULL, hein? What do these PAYMENTS refer to though? Ah, street life! In other words, "everyday life." Must be nice to be part of this everyday life, and observe Greek Myths being refracted. There's Hephaestus, rocking on his front porch in Iron City. Frisky is a foreman down at the plant. He has a florid face, and an ugly birthmark that spreads across his forehead, shaped like an anvil. He has the bends. He has a daughter—Constance—"Con" for short. Silly Con is what the boss calls her when he brings them their roast pig on the 4th of July, and he winks at Frisky sympathetically. His wife is Apple Diet. That's what everyone calls her, smilingly. She won't eat anything but apples. She sticks some apples in the voluminous pockets of her nightie, and goes to the attic to open her hope chest. Inside is her honeymoon nightie. She feels it lovingly, against the smoothness of her cheeks. It becomes evident to me that they don't quite refract, these Greek Myths.

So I obliterate the thuds and shrieks of shells across the border by recalling mother whispering as she pulls the curtains against the bad night air, how her gown rustles against the tile floor of the bathroom as she goes to the sink to pour water into the glass she will later place on the bedside table, and now we are much older, it is our psychological bride Diana Vienna, carefully putting the glass on the metal table without making a sound, no, it is our daughter, we are old and ill, so insensate we cannot remember her name, Vivienna, much less move our arms, so we clench a pencil between our teeth and write on the starched white coverlet: KILL ME, NO, we aren't functioning so well of late, we meant: COOL ME. She is puzzled by our eye motion (right to left, eye shuts, opens, right to left again) till she notices the message, she understands before we do what we wanted all along, a glass of water. She bends down and tips the glass towards our lips, we sip, a pause, we sip, a pause—we feel like those toys in drugstore windows, those toy birds so popular in the not so recent past, birds that clenched the rim of the glass in their claws, and dipped their beaks into the water, only to—aha! We are now able to hear a memory of a certain past rustling, whispering to us more clearly than we have the right to expect under such conditions—how fortunate, to be able to impose a design on ordinary air, in flux, by recalling past air, the way it rustled the trees in a lulling way, its smells and motions, how it grew foggy that morning, and upset us when we cawed and cawed like crows at dawn do, that morning, to scare it, the air, out of revenge for cloaking the sun in fog, and then clawed it, like an angry jaguar rending its prey, that morning, when we were a child: too small to reach the bullets on the belt of the soldier standing on the striped cement pavement just beyond the store where mother, Diana

Vienna, and Vivienna go to buy us cake and fresh eggs
and star-shaped cookies, which, seated around the bed,
they proceed to devour, noisily smacking their lips with
enjoyment, much to our satisfaction. In such a situation,
when, to repeat, one is afraid of the endlessness of it, no?—
one is likely simply to freeze, like a wild animal aware it's
being observed, hoping to merge with the landscape; but
the landscape is likely to be the opposite of the landscape
one is accustomed to—or one wouldn't be in such a
situation in the first place.

"Hi! . . . diddle . . . horse . . . Sam . . . Beth-Annie-
Lou . . . Fulda's—"

Very dark looks are being exchanged. Fulda's? FULDA'S?
This is Texas after all, cactus phenomena in the dawn,
hydrofarms, flatness. It's only human, when surrounded
by such flatness, to recall cold Swiss Alps, where the
villagers carry shepherd's crooks on feastdays, not guns,
where everyone is financially independent due to the fore-
sight of frugal forebears who kept within severe budgetary
restrictions in order to live on the interest of the interest
of their investments in mildly war-torn areas. Everyone
devotes many enjoyable hours to keeping journals—of the
weather, sleepy churchly doings, border disputes in the
outside world, chores, tomes, hymns, sunsets, charades,
hikes, hand-me-downs handed down, reunions, accounts
of profits (and expenditures), and in code, at the bottom
of the page, fleeting references to debts, semen deposits,
deaths. No need to claw at the air, to rend it like a jaguar.
One simply reaches up with chubby fingers, and squeezing
it hard, milks it! Plenty for everyone! Even though no
sky designs last, frozen into reliability, one feels free on
good days to cut out as big chunks of sky (or air—take
your pick . . . those very same people who do not cotton
to any mention of "Fulda" in the same breath with "Beth-

Annie-Lou" will forgive you if you mention "sky chunks"
as opposed to "air chunks"—please be sure to pronounce
"chunks" so it doesn't get off into "chinks"—that'll
frighten them, but good!—and they'll retreat into their
air-conditioned limousines, and zoom away, back onto the
traffic cube, babbling of "Fu Manchu" and "doo-dads"—
which is their quaint way of saying "torture") as one
dares, and to pull them along, muscles aching, sometimes
improvising a wooden cart with sharp metallic pushers
and prods to help transport this welcome burden to its
final resting place: namely, anywhere you want to dump
it when you're tired of lugging it around. All of which one
doesn't necessarily bother doing, for one hates to miss out
on the new chunks all around one, waiting patiently or
impatiently, as the case may be. On bad days, or even
so-so neutral days, they generally mind their own business,
and one is free to remain indoors, in a curtained room,
whispering to oneself, KILL ME, waiting to see if a glass of
water will magically appear. It doesn't, which reinforces
one's belief in a messy, pseudo-democratic reality, where
good hard work is rewarded by just plain survival, with
lots of honest appraisal going on, self-appraisal too—that's
how one lops off unnecessary appendages (monocles, toi-
lets, electric fences, ferris wheels, art galleries, cinder
blocks, wrist alarms) in order to remain functional.

In such a situation, surrounded by Texan flatness, one
wonders, "What to do with my sky chunks? Dump them
under hard western sunlight, until deep cracks appear,
cracks that widen into fissures, fissures that widen into
abysses with frail frayed rope-bridges spanning them every
fifty miles or so? Wouldn't it be advisable, having dumped
the old chunks, to steer clear of new ones, even on good
days, and thus regain an old lightness long since lost—a

lightness that might enable me to arrive back at a happy and familiar starting point, surrounded by well-wishers and hopes for the future?"

Hopes. Hopes for a future devoid of tunnels that lead to attics, with cubes outside, and silos, and down the pike, dance-hall dames, with oldsters, pills, rhapsodies?

With a little patience and ingenuity, a starting point can easily be transformed into a circle in which one can stay put, if you balloon it up a little, under one, and by tracing out a normal-sized wedge, whatever feels comfortable, you get a whole new circumference, with you at the center. If you aren't bothered by memories of the wedge lines, once you've consciously erased them, you can stay put. Empty? Yes, bet your ass. Permanent? Maybe. By these means, one can avail oneself of the living and breathing presences around one, more fully, this time, especially by kindling a non-stop fire, which is not only a valuable visual aid, it's nice for passing strangers, grappling with their very own individual loss of lightness. The stupid urgency that nuances assume (if you don't hear the crackling twig, the monster with the slimy tongue will—that's the big question) is distanced, enabling one to hang on to the full picture going on around one. Initiations lose their urgency too, and fade into the picture faster than they otherwise would. A certain tension does hang over one (like a greedy fat vehicle that lives on air, sky, what have you, and is devouring it at a 2–4–16 etc. ratio) while one cultivates as much peaceful sameness as one can, innocently, underneath. One asks passing visitor-strangers for matches, newspapers, carefully avoiding a glance at the headlines. It's not the time to be distracted by accident vertigos hundreds of miles away—a bonfire! This accomplished, the circle widens voraciously, at a 2–4–16 etc. ratio, racing the fat vehicle that lives on air, sky, what have you. A whole new tension. A race! More and more passing visitor-strangers are drawn by this prospect of permanence and intimacies that only begin to flourish after long periods of tranquillity and mutual trust. At which point, the prospects of the morrow expand into infinite clutter. The visitor-strangers sense that the air is full of tension. More effort is required to achieve the goal of—of peaceful permanence, flourishing intimacies. More fires. The race must be won. Other fires and other circles proliferate, other centers, it's very exciting, the speed of everything, the lack of darkness, no time for sleep, if only one didn't feel so depressed at so much effort going down the drain, for there is very little air left now, the bonfire and the circle seem a long time ago, for one has surely been in this closet for quite a spell, with the fat circus freak lady who unloosened her stays after locking the door, which is odd—a closet that can be locked on the inside. Her rolls of fat push out and out, pressing one against the closet wall—you'd think she'd have a bigger closet for her spangled costumes and all, for her cloaks, and tiaras, and jodhpurs for riding the elephant side-saddle. She is rapacious, and now one feels someone else's breath on one's elbow, warm breath anyway, three in one closet —you'd think she'd have a bigger closet for her social engagements and all—if only one hadn't lit that fire and started the 2–4–16 etc. ratio . . . her voice. It grates so, as she explains about "the third party," as she calls him, it is a male then, he is a "breath freak"—her phrase—he cannot differentiate between breathing and sexual congress—move your elbow a bit his way, bub, have a heart—she is very moral about his predilection though—"didn't trundle his air fat fast enough"—by which she means "sky chunks" —"that's what happens, gotta keep a weather eye out for the new air fat truckin' on down the old pikeroodydoody"—he's breathed again, lightly on my elbow. They're not bad sorts, that's for sure.

In such a situation, surrounded by Texa—grrr! Swiss Swiss Swiss. Swiss mountains—Alps, Alps. Yes, here in the Alps, the morning withers. It goes down hill. It starts out fresh, and gets progressively more saggy, and when it's all puffy and flaccid and mottled, it turns into afternoon. Afternoon: same deal. Dusk: same deal. Something to figure out here, relating to SOUTHS. Nations, going from north to south, do the same. They start out all bright, tight-fisted and rarin' to go (north) and end up saggy and sloppy-drunk and slatternly (south)—what needs figuring out is why Nation A's SOUTH which is north of Nation B's NORTH, is saggy and sloppy drunk and slatternly, while Nation B's NORTH, south of Nation A's SOUTH, is bright, tight-fisted and rarin' to go. This new concern of mine is a trifle academic, hein? Especially as it's well-nigh impossible to get a decent fix on the morning, much less any available souths or norths, in the immediate vicinity of the area I seem restricted to: closet. They say the louvers of the village lower and raise according to the sun's intensity. This info is courtesy The Breather, who's turning into a regular chatterbox.

"You mean LOVERS of the village, ha ha ha?"—my first riposte.

He lapses into an injured silence. The fat lady's no help in pepping things up—she's fast asleep, sprawled across my middle and lower extremities, which are asleep too: numb asleep. His pique passes soon enough—he's a regular authority on louvers. Jan–Mar: windy. Apr–Jun: windy. Jul–Sep: windy. Oct–Dec: windy. The louvers don't stop the bitter wind from the glacier. All year, the locals stomp, curse, bite their fingers just to feel something hot,

even if it is acute pain. The locals say a warm city lies
'neath the glacier. One reaches it by means of a cave. The
cave lies beyond a five-sided wheat-field and another five-
sided wheat-field. One must beware of the burgeoning
leaves—they unfold suddenly, pressing one against old
barbed wire: they are disgustingly sticky—one must be-
ware of the burgeoning leaves. The Breather's an authority
on louvers and leaves too, it seems. And on the best, safest
route. One must find the signposts by keeping to the high
places, above the leaves. One must bank on glimpsing the
stone tops of the posts when the leaves are motionless,
in between gusts of glacier wind: that's how one must
find the signposts. How seductive the shade under the
leaves must be. One sleeps surrounded by growth, con-
stant growth—the lulling whispers of stalks reaching
toward one to tickle one gently on the elbow. How se-
ductive the shade under the leaves must be. He takes the
hint, breathes. A new silence. He must be mulling over
this adventure in reciprocation. One awakes. The city is
all around one. One trudges past parking lots, hotels,
factories—one makes inquiries, but no one has heard of
any wheat-fields, much less a cave, though there once was
a glacier, but it melted years ago—a lagoon is there now,
with row boats and a place to buy ice cream and various
liquid refreshments, and beyond it, an amusement park—
THE COMBINE. The way to the central plaza is pointed
out, where ensconced on a tower is a clock the city is
inordinately proud of, with a five-sided wheat-field man
and a five-sided wheat-field woman who twirl and hug
each other at noon. Two identical doors open, way up.
Out they come; they twirl and hug at a middle point.
The five-sided wheat-field man jiggles and bounces.
Wheat-field man collapses. Wheat-field woman returns to
upright position. So does he. All over! The burghers and

tourists disperse before the doors on the tower clang shut—that is not what they came for. Such pleasant traffic! Trucks mosey along, trucks of all sorts and sizes. A shame The Breather isn't with me: what admirable directions he gave, but it's no longer interesting to hunt for caves and underground cities and warmth. Time to see THE COMBINE. There's the fat lady, on a blue chair on a plat-form—she doesn't look so bad in the daylight.

"How happy I am to see you!"

"Your costume is magnificent."

"The old times . . ."

"And The Breather?"

"He's in my trailer this very minute."

The drivers are leaning out of their cabs to catch the shafts of sunlight in between the dark patches of shadow—so many trestles and girders. Soon they'll roll up their windows for the trek across the mountains, heading for the plains to the south, where it's always morning, if one keeps heading south fast enough. In the last truck, crouched in excelsior-packed crates marked FAUTEUIL is: the blond soldier with the mustache and the Sarge and Ypra. They have bought a vineyard, Ypra and the soldier, with money the Sarge has given them as a wedding present —just in time, too, as Ypra's belly is already swelling. Ypra plans to get a job as a telephone switchboard operator in the hilltown near the vineyard, and the Sarge has some ideas about what to grow—hidden among the grapes. He and the youth with the blond mustache may have to spend considerable time in the cities together, working out satis-factory business arrangements for their produce. They are partners—50–50—all the way up and down the line. Ypra won't be lonely, with the baby to look after, and, for company, she'll have the Fat Lady and The Breather,

who are looking forward to retiring from the hurly-burly
of circus life. They are in the truck too, in a larger crate
marked FAUTEUIL. Up front, unaware of the human cargo
in back, Diana Vienna and Barry sit, enjoying the sights,
with me at the wheel, anxious to dispense with the formali-
ties at the border, so I can get onto the rounding the leaf
traffic cube just across the border, beyond the guard with
bullets in his belt, waving for us to stop, at the edge of
the zebra-striped pavement, across which the men with
the machine guns are clomping—terrible thumping sounds.
They are banging the back door of the truck—clomp
clomp clomp—the three of us sit, motionless—the angle
of the windshield wiper and the palm tree ahead alters.
The raised leg of the black chow urinating on it is now
below the wiper. Before it was above. The guards wave
us on. Once past the border, I look through the peephole,
into the back of the truck. As I expected, empty of
furniture.

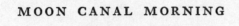

MOON CANAL MORNING

1. *On The Screen-o-phone*

"—another continent—"

"—Mummers Memorial Info-Surround Environment Junction—specializing in any available infra-relationships between air, weather, orchids, traffic cubes, explorers, family ties, simultaneity nightmares, sex garb, and 'breath pulse.'"

So much static. Weavy red lines. Dyed hair tossing?

"—my function is to keep a record of incoming and outgoing info-surrounds, how everyone's research is progressing, and to keep a sharp look-out for mis-info, you know—sabotage! All of which makes it so thrilling! What a challenge, being an effective clearinghouse regulator, hein? Yesterday I decided to put the Mummers Info-Surround on the map. So many requests to overloaded environment junctions could be directed my way, thereby avoiding inadvertent chaos. To be honest, whole days go by without one outside feeler. Today I found out my three-pronged plan has been rejected. First prong: subliminal foto-clusters on traffic cube info-surrounds, ones near urban retirement-and-death sectors, showing Environment Comptrollers gathered in our main sensory digest area. One feeds another a grape, and before you know it, his hand is exploring the mouth, nothing fetid, but you sense there's considerable rapport between them, and in the background, which consists of a blue sky, you see this slogan I thought up by myself, being pulled by a dirigible, a banner—

WANDER THROUGH THE SKY RID OF INVENTIONS
CHINA WISDOM WEALTH AND OLDER DISEASES FREE
OF THE LAW OF CREATION: ABANDON NATURE—
THIS MESSAGE IS THANKS TO THE MUMMERS MEMORIAL
INFO-SURROUND ENVIRONMENT JUNCTION
OF SUNSHINE TEXAS—YOURS DIANA VIENNA!"

Weavy red lines. More static. Cucumber-shaped face.

"Second prong: same slogan on all factory roofs, for at least three minutes at dusk, when the Environment Comptrollers are heading home in their hydroplanes, weary but suggestible—"

Hard to believe! Right there on the viewer—just about my main ecstasy source (in human form)—Diana Vienna.

2. *Blue Sack*

A throbbing filled the air. I peered out the window of my bedroom. A Blue Silo Hydroplane approached directly overhead. Its shadow almost blotted out the ten-lane traffic cube rising just beyond the serrated roof of the Wingate Barn.

Two blue ropes were let down, with hooks at regular intervals on their interior sides. The shrill throbbing of the motors above was deafening, and a fierce wind beat against the side of the barn, exposing the silvery undersides of the leaves of a grove of espaliered peach trees.

A blue sack dropped down out of a square opening between the hydroplane's landing discs—rather like a trapdoor in a distant ceiling, through which one could climb into an attic with an eye-shaped window. The sack wavered from side to side, and landed on the lawn gently, as the blue ropes receded into the sky. It was positioned directly in front of a tunnel beneath Barry Wingate's sleeping quarters.

3. *Swinson Glance Technique*

Only the week before, Barry had completed his first psycho-surround, the day of my arrival, and had taken it over to Sunshine, Texas, to the Mummers Memorial Junction for examination. Diana Vienna fed *DELIA* into three slots: WEATHER, FAMILY TIES, and SEX GARB. The results were "go," so she submitted it immediately to the local Environment Comptrollers. They agreed to process it for release during the 11 A.M.–3 P.M. traffic lull. Drivers and passengers alike on the Sunshine Traffic Cube could absorb its 117 frames and 14 foto-clusters in under 2 minutes, moving at the normal speed, and using the Swinson Glance Technique as follows:

> *Right to left, eye shuts, opens,*
> *right to left again. Images project*
> *on underside of eyelid while eye*
> *moves (shut) from left to right*
> *to complete subliminal glance cycle.*

4. DELIA

FRAMES

1. Delia and Tom, a young post-war farm couple
2. (Indian corn dolls manipulated by yellow hands
3. with long silvered fingernails), move around
4. their mobile home making breakfast. It goes
5. around curve, and a cup falls to the floor—
6. bounces back up high enough for Tom to catch
7. it. He presents it to her with a bow.
8. Delia puts the toast in the toaster. Tom
9. makes scrambled eggs and bacon, brews coffee
10. in the percolator, and squeezes orange juice.
11. Delia butters the toast, and sets the table.
12. She gives Tom a backrub as he's busy cooking,
13. standing behind him. Another curve catches
14. them off guard—they lose their balance.

FOTO-CLUSTERS

1. *Silo-shaped bottles standing in rows in*
2. *field begin marching out of fields in*
3. *military formation, down country lane, two-by-*
4. *two. Ice-cubes float in air above them,*
5. *cheering them on. City shines in distance.*

FRAMES

15. They start falling.

16. They continue falling.

17. They continue falling.

18. They continue falling.

19. They continue falling.

20. They continue falling.

21. They continue falling.

22. Tom reaches the floor.

23. Delia reaches the floor.

24. They lie on the floor.

25. They lie on the floor.

26. They lie on the floor.

27. They lie on the floor.

28. Delia tries to get up and fails.

29. Delia tries to get up and fails.

30. Delia tries to get up and fails.

31. Delia tries to get up and fails.

32. Tom tries to get up and fails.

33. Tom tries to get up and fails.

34. Tom tries to get up and fails.

35. Tom tries to get up and fails.

36. Tom touches Delia.

37. Tom touches Delia.

38. Tom touches Delia.

39. Tom touches Delia.

40. A newspaper flies in through the window.

41. A newspaper flies in through the window.

42. A newspaper lands on the floor.

43. A newspaper lands on the floor.

44. A newspaper lands on the floor.

45. Delia pushes Tom's hand away.

46. Delia reaches for the newspaper.

47. Tom pushes Delia's hand away.
48. Tom reaches for the newspaper.
49. Tom reaches for the newspaper.
50. Tom looks at a photograph.
51. Tom looks at a photograph.
52. Photograph: a smiling runner with a silver cup.
53. Photograph: a smiling runner with a silver cup.
54. Photograph: a smiling runner with a silver cup on an ocean liner.
55. Photograph: a smiling runner with a silver cup on an ocean liner.
56. Photograph: on the dock, a massed regiment of black troops. Fezzes.
57. Photograph: on the dock, a massed regiment of black troops. Fezzes.
58. Tom turns the page.
59. Tom turns the page.
60. Tom turns the page.
61. Photograph: some old men huddled under a bridge, cooking soup.
62. Photograph: some old men huddled under a bridge, cooking soup.
63. Photograph: over the bridge, a freight-train is speeding.
64. Photograph: over the bridge, a freight-train is speeding.
65. Photograph: a freight-train carrying convertibles is speeding.
66. Photograph: a freight-train carrying convertibles is speeding.
67. Tom looks down the page.
68. Tom looks down the page.

69. Delia points at the page.
70. Delia points at the page.
71. Delia points at the page.
72. Photograph: a blossoming tree, with a sap bucket on its trunk.
73. Photograph: a blossoming tree, with a sap bucket on its trunk.
74. Photograph: two girls in bathing-suits on each side of the tree.
75. Photograph: two girls in bathing-suits on each side of the tree.

FOTO-CLUSTERS

6. *Silo-shaped bottles march past the blossoming tree,*
7. *as the two girls hold up a floral tribute to General*
8. *"Gemman" Joe. The ice-cubes follow overhead, and the*
9. *spires of the city appear. The bottles pass an old*
10. *woman on a lawn in a black peasant dress. A square*
11. *needlepoint rug is draped over her lap—a portrait*
12. *of a U. S. Savings Bond. A U.S. sailor, marine, and*
13. *doughboy stand saluting behind her. An Oriental is*
14. *pushing a lawn-mower. The bottles march on and on.*

FRAMES

76. Tom turns the page.
77. Tom turns the page.
78. Tom turns the page.
79. Delia points.
80. Delia points.
81. Photograph: a snow-covered mountain.
82. Photograph: a snow-covered mountain.
83. Photograph: a snow-covered mountain with a stream running down.
84. Photograph: a snow-covered mountain with a stream running down.
85. Photograph: steam curls up into the sky from the stream.
86. Photograph: steam curls up into the sky from the stream.
87. Photograph: four men in trenchcoats are standing near the stream.
88. Photograph: four men in trenchcoats are standing near the stream.
89. Photograph: a girl in a bathing-suit is sitting in the stream.
90. Photograph: a girl in a bathing-suit is sitting in the stream.
91. Photograph: a girl in a bathing-suit is waving to the four men.
92. Photograph: a girl in a bathing-suit is waving to the four men.
93. Delia grabs the paper.
94. Delia grabs the paper.
95. She gets up.
96. She gets up.
97. She gets up.

98. She gets up.

99. Tom gets up.

100. Tom gets up.

101. Tom gets up.

102. Tom gets up.

103. Delia opens a soft-drink (Blue Silo).

104. Delia opens a soft-drink (Blue Silo).

105. Delia opens a soft-drink (Blue Silo).

106. She pours the liquid into two glasses.

107. She pours the liquid into two glasses.

108. She pours the liquid into two glasses.

109. Tom sits down to table.

110. Tom sits down to table.

111. Delia hands Tom a glass of Blue Silo.

112. Delia hands Tom a glass of Blue Silo.

113. Delia sits down.

114. Delia sits down.

115. Tom drinks some Blue Silo.

116. Tom drinks some Blue Silo.

117. Tom drinks some Blue Silo.

5. *The Advent Of The Hooded Figure*

I closed my eyes and saw a thought cube vision:

> limousine on a dead-end road
> with a chauffeur standing be
> side it scanning tree-top ne
> rvously or is he merely scan
> ning a dirigible—sky ad w
> ith great brand-names slante
> d towards the sun. One touc
> h of darkness—delicate bl
> ack lines like tendrils in a
> tropical vine tactfully hidd

"—vetoed the idea, but I do have permission to embark on a new project—performances of a personality envelope builder upper, *MOON CANAL MORNING*, assembled by Gertrud Schmidlapp herself. I've thought of a three-pronged plan to really put it on the map! First prong, subliminal foto-clusters—"

Barry Wingate walked out of the tunnel. He took hold of the sack, and dragged it into the tunnel. Seconds later, he emerged, walked to the barn, and took his windbreaker off. He began feeding dried corn into a genuine antique farm machine. Kernels of corn spewed into a pail, making clattery noises. The shorn ears dropped into a gunnysack attached to the side of the barn.

"—third prong, throwaway leaflets on zeps, hydros, even the congloms, to establish rapport—"

A hooded figure peeked around the corner of the barn. The figure straightened up, and inched along the side of the barn, keeping to the morning shadows. The hooded figure stood, flattened against the barn. The hooded figure lit up a cigarette. Dust granules and roof coolant follicles were whirling around the lawn, like aerial insect cities, agitated by the exhaust of the now distant Blue Silo Hydroplane.

6. THE ATHLETE AND THE HOBO

The day before, I'd started work on a full-length psycho-surround of my own, egged on by Barry's success. How I longed to encounter Diana Vienna in some semi-official capacity that would recreate our reading the steam camaraderie! A camaraderie that would set in motion an old-fashioned color scramble: whoosh, whoosh, ba-ta-ta-bzzzzzz! Ah, wondrous unity—admittedly fragile, like a landscape full of dumb animals looking for shelter, dumb because they're sniffing for the smell of trees (no trees), the odor of honeysuckle vines (no vines), the stench of open man-holes in the city (no city), the nauseating stink of crumbling stone wet by streams (no streams, no stone) —there it goes! An ecstasy cube—into a tunnel—a Diana cube—other one catches up—now if they can only get together—second one swoops into tunnel—the "me" cube —no control over it—first one's looped back—snooping

—dives in after second one—half in one tunnel and half in other—split down middle—skitters back out into the sun and joins up with itself—second one emerges all bent —both flatten out—disappear—whoosh, whoosh—chase— daredevils—many a near miss—they careen, twist, sensing ahead of time random gusts of wind—

Barry handed me a copy of that day's *HYDROFARM DREAMS & EVENTS*—the local journal. The dreams of the locals were turned into fotos, along with important events, and the juxtaposition of the two, and the resultant guessing which was which was a popular pastime in the area: the publication's circulation was zooming. Barry'd culled material from it for his *DELIA*; I followed suit, and in no time, I'd hit on a story line:

An athlete is given a big send-off from his fatherland, Liberia. The big day depresses him, for his father is nothing but a hobo. He gets off the boat, and searches for his father, finding him under a bridge, drinking soup.

That's as far as I got. I noticed a foto on Page 5. A pretty girl was sitting on the lap of an old, old man. A woman was handing the girl a cocktail. Another woman was lighting the girl's cigarette. The women were buxom: Gertrud and Helga. The old, old man was Dr. Schmidlapp. A dirigible in the sky pulled a banner that announced the grand opening of the Mummers Memorial Info-Surround Environment Junction. The girl was Diana Vienna.

7. *The Take Off*

"—basic Icelandic, aided by Helga, who is—hein, hein—
the ex-Mrs. Schmidlapp. I've had a go at the translation.
In fact, I'll read it to you right now. Now I'm unzipping
it. My valise is propped against my chair, see? See? Taking
translation out. Just touching it makes me feel good. Now
I've opened the translation to Page 1. So excited! Excuse
me, I have to freshen my coffee . . ."

The static stopped. I could see the empty chair, and
the open valise propped beside it.

I looked down at the valise propped against the chair
I'd sleep-walked to. In it lay (unopened) my "Holy City
Geography Book," given to me by Barry, upon my ar-
rival—a real welcome. Any day now, so he promised,
he'd tell me the combination on the valise's lock. And
any day now, construction would begin, so he promised,
to convert the area above my room into an attic, with an
eye-shaped window, and with skeletal stairs . . .

I looked up. Attack of "trapdoor-itis"—nostalgia for
the "Native Innards" box reposing back in Hode . . .

*Wisps. Streaks. Puffing up. Laser vibrations
constricted on my thumb-nail. Instant intensity!
Circles in assorted colors widen—steady flow.
Hurts my eyes. Circles widen. Streaming out of
my thumb. My thumb isn't my usual thumb. My
thumb is energy source (must sabotage laser beam
vibration circles) fanning out over trees. Put my
thumb in my mouth (pressing edge of nail against
roof of mouth, hard). Great lungings and
wheelings well up. Swallow. Echoed grunts of
pleasure. Happy throbbings. Hein, hein. They
quicken. They connect. Dribbles of sound
spinning around me like ectoplasm goobers. Fan
out. Bump against obstacle. "Scuse." Screamy
though: "SCUSE." SCUSE! Streaks start to get
tangled. IN me. Matted. Open mouth, out they
lunge. Turn into sound dribbles that start to come
from someone else. Dribbles puff up into scream.
Solid scream, not on or off or it dies down.
Keeps replenishing itself effortlessly. Like sitting
in a tepid bath. Watching redden. Redden and
darken. What redden and darken? Water redden
and darken. In the water—*

streaks   wisps of   "linear essentials"
wingless gray insects one-eighth of inch
tanks had wonderful—thrip
semi-transparent a
pierces tiss

spittoon   license plates   eye-shaped window
reflected in it   me in tub of water (red)
water   keeps replenishing it
effortlessly   nice for
the scream change
into bath

sitting in tepid bath   watching water redden and
darken only to realize one is peeing out
pleasantly a never-ending supply
of one's own lifeblood
City Foam chunks
autombol
FOU

8. *Son Of Thunder Story*

Something about Barry's back reminded me of Harry Black, a hack-driver who'd driven us past great cactus phenomena in the dawn, followed by great blue silos in the distance (hydrofarms) the day of my arrival in Texas. While Barry and I had dozed, stretched out full-length on the back seat, Harry Black's voice had woven soothingly in and out of my newfangled fold-ins and old-fashioned color scrambles as we zoomed along, stretched out naked in the curtained chamber, two jiggling spoons in a waterproof pouch, hurtling over Niagara Falls—back to Harry Black!

Blue Silo.	"went	to	Fort	L"
Blue Silo.	"ex-Zep		pardner"
Blue Silo.	"suck	duck,	yup"
Blue Silo.	"pink	dink,	pup"
Blue Silo.	"Glory	Hole	Cal"
Blue Silo.	"tongue		through"
Blue Silo.	"bigwig		buggery"
Blue Silo.	"drove	back	Cal"
Blue Silo.	"be	a	threesome"
Blue Silo.	"come	in,	kiddo"
Blue Silo.	"fled	back	to	Y"
Blue Silo.	"TV	set	on,	eek"
Blue Silo.	"shoe		squashing"
Blue Silo.	"hypodermic	. . .	I"
Blue Silo.	"take	off	duds!"
Blue Silo.	"john	door	open"
Blue Silo.	"Fat	Peak	Woman"
Blue Silo.	"hikes	up	skirt"
Blue Silo.	"wal	if	it	aint"
Blue Silo.	"SON OF THUNDER"

Hard to marshal the exact sequence of events, that moon canal morning, but, judging from transitory image reconstructions, plus rounding the leaf awareness there in that chair, valise right beside me, my hand stroking the lock—

Anyway, it was 9:22 when Barry took off his shirt and hung it on the machine. Blue Silo.

9. *Moon Canal Morning*

At 9:23, Diana Vienna launched into Gertrud Schmidlapp's personality envelope builder upper. The weavy red lines thickened, but I could hear her sip her coffee, now and again, as she paused for breath.

"Chime. Doorbell. Bong bong bong. Slam of door from above. Ladies voices. Steps on the stairs above. Someone trips. Mutual laughter. Whoop whoop whoop. Ah, Helga is discovered as the klieg lights flash on, leaning against a washing machine, world-weary smile on her face. Helga is a sparrow with bits of stolen eyebrow pencils in her nest, and a stolen stick to buff her tarantula legs to a fine sheen, so she can find her way, one day, to a hall of mirrors, heated mirrors, the better to stare at the glints her leg hair makes in candlelight, which, in the crossfire of reflections, reminds her of night pilgrims in Spanish valleys far below, their candles reflected on the surfaces of their crutches, braces, wheelchairs. She also recalls dawn-of-history winters, so it doesn't alarm her one bit how foxes gnaw at the bones, the bones (it is now a modern springtime) of her habitual procedures, in plain English, skulls, dotting the mesa—and, dear colleague, if you ask about the skulls, she has a malicious Prussian way of saying yes, so you feel like a pushy serf with no code of honor. Soon the Earth as we know it will pass through a sapphire phase, and in that blue future, Blue Future (the klieg lights dim here, as a shadowy Gertrud advances towards the washing machine), you'll find Gertrud a tower of lavender ice, glittering like tinted diamonds in a monument of newer ice that protects the Gertrud Tower from hot bird saliva and hot bird droppings and hot bird embryos dripping with bird tears and sweat. Bong bong bong. Gertrud extends her hand. Helga takes Gertrud's hand with a must-we-be-so-formal shooting up of her eyebrows. Helga pecks Gertrud on the cheek, and pumps her hand up and down. Loud BZZZ. BZZZZZZ. Gertrud doubles over with whoop whoop whoop sounds, and wipes tears of laughter from her eyes."

10. *Steel-blue Claw In The Harbor*

Gertrud: *Whoop whoop whoop. Here, Helga. Let me*
            show you my wolf ring.

Helga: *Yes, a little Mozart would be most soothing.*

Gertrud: *Wolf ring, I said—wolf RING. It has ruby*
            eyes, see, genuine ivory fangs, a malachite
            tongue, sterling silver fur, chased. It's hollow.
            My wedding ring. Bend down close so you can
            inculcate the fangs.

Helga: *What—amusement death? Amusement death?*

Gertrud: *Amusement death? Amusement death? I'll have*
            you know I'm happily married. Yes, to your
            ex-husband, yes. Amusement death? Now I
            scare you. Bend down, Helga!

Helga: *This luncheon—this basement—the fangs—*

Gertrud: *Bend down instantly.*

Helga: *If you say so.*

Gertrud: *I do say so.*

Helga: *Ach. Liquid's coming out of your ring. Fangs—*

Gertrud: *Whoop whoop whoop.*

Helga: *Hola! My Algerian politico. My customary*
            saunter. I found myself in a blue desert, resting
            on a pink roof. Fellatio! The hogs in that
            grass-roofed market . . . the gutters! My shoes

. . . the plane to Zurich left with no me aboard.
A thin needle of silver could be seen arising in
the distant black mountains. The invaders were
waiting to pounce on our defenseless city.
Striped straws were jutting out of the sand.
An old-fashioned color scramble! A camel sat
down. It was pierced. Drained. Saggy humps,
some fur left to bake in the blue desert. How
frolicsome the French girls seemed on the
beach of the dinky suburb, tumbling down the
dunes, clambering back up. Hola! A silver
needle rose out of the surf. The girls lay down
and told lovely spectre stories. They slept, their
black lashes fluttering as they dreamt, much as
the legs of racing dogs twitch as they see (a
dream scramble) grandstand vacationers (ochre
to puce)—flamingo legs (terra cotta to khaki)
—pennants (mustard to olive drab). The straws,
hola! Too late. Poor limp things. What is the
custom? Should I—about burial—the skins
might blow away—notify the proper—I'm in
the station: camel, dunes, girls. They laugh.
The Sergeant indulges in louche raillery—down
to business. He hands me the business card of
a well-to-do Brazilian, a certain Mr. Chicago
Honduras—a mint tea with him at midnight,
that is all that is required of me, and I will be
exonerated. Exonerated? Hola! Chicago's terra
cotta lips disgust me. I run to the hotel. So
little call for my glass paintings of city fires
and holocausts. Too much of the real thing all
around. And so little food. Resentment of us
mixed-bloods. The manager thrust the door

open. I was in my scanties. Take my shoes to
be cleaned, there's a good man. Telegram,
madame. Telegram for me? My politico says:
join me. A famous city, begins with a—a—hola,
a Z, a Z. Champagne? A celebration is in order,
but perhaps you could inform me, those needles
on the rooftops glittering in the sun, outside
the window—. He lies down on my bed.
Nosebleed. Straws, straws, smashing the
windows . . . woozy . . . do something, I
shouted. The steel-blue claw in the harbor,
liberation! Sand flies at dusk, I thought as I
came to. No, it was the injection, given me by
the kindly hooded figure. The first words I said
were: MUSIC BY CANDLELIGHT.

Gertrud: I'm afraid we have neither candles nor music
for this luncheon festivity. Let's eat. I'm
starved. I cannot, absolutely cannot comprehend
in regards to you.

11. *9:39*

Hooded figure taps Barry on the shoulder. He lets out a
fake yowl, and then bends down to kiss hooded figure. Kiss.
MMMMMMMMM sound. Hooded figure's right hand
brushes Barry's chest with forefinger—one arch per breast.
Left hand makes upside-down T pattern, MMMMM,
along belt, up to stomach button.   *SMALL THOUGHT*
Right hand: figure 8, horizontal,   *CUBE VISION*
                                              ROOFS
so each nipple is center of hole,
of the circles of the 8. Also—   *wending its*
right hand makes whirling motions   *way past va*
                                           st roofs wi
in hollow of Barry's stomach but-   *th great br*
ton, like corkscrew driving in. A   *and-names s*
fast zigzag up to throat comes next, and a poke at his
Adam's apple—then a repeat of entire sequence—hori-
zontal 8, stomach button whirl, zigzag poke. Left hand
keeps making upside-down T, MMMMMMM, toys with
belt. Fingers move like a crab scrabbling for shelter—

12. *Washing Machine Fold-in*

Wouldn't mind if Gertrud and Helga were feeding bananas to Diana Vienna. Their hair could be up in plastic pink curlers—they could be listening to records, in a Barry-and-me intimate way. We wait on table, Barry-and-me, at a tea-shop frequented by widows with a predilection for the Occult. Thing is, it's Saturday, and the washing machine is on the blink, and our dotted Swiss print frocks are in it, and our boy-friends, Hal and Mack, who work in a garage in the next town, are expected to come by to pick us up for a drive in an old-fashioned electric automobile. Gertrud isn't bothered by accident vertigo, but we are, Barry-and-me. Mrs. Thurber, the owner of the car, has gone to the seaside for some sun, but she's given us permission to use it in her absence. Bong Bong Bong. They're here, Diana Vienna says. What'll we do? Gertrud and Helga get the giggles at this. They let the boys in. Behave, Gertrud says. They explain their predicament. We need those print frocks to go dancing. Hal and Mack volunteer to fix the washing machine— can't be too different from a regular automobile. Hal pokes his head in, gets drenched. Sopping wet Sunday best suit. Mack says, lemme. Sopping wet too. Gertrud's on the floor, whoop whoop whoop—confesses she wired it on purpose. Let's get out of these wet things, Hal says. Soon he's down to his jockey shorts. Whoop whoop whoop, Helga and Diana Vienna are doing it too. The lights go out. Gertrud really has hysterics now: WHOOP WHOOP WHOOP. Now we're in a heap on the floor, in the dark. What a tangle, arms, legs, breasts, hair, noses, lips, elbows—try as they may, they can't stop laughing down there.

13. *9:43 Lecture*

Gaps, gaps, gaps.

I gave myself quite a lecture—have delusion I'm tourist passing through colorful foreign land full of delightful natives I must make psycho-surrounds of, perpetuating amusing phrases and contretemps for some future or other—all very fine to stare out of dirigible window (eyes)—a few days later it's gone, all gone. The ticket-taker waving the dirigible on and up, the old lady selling fruit, the soldier bidding his sweetheart goodbye, she's pregnant, the gardener watering the mimosa the town is proud of—a charming plaza can be seen next to the airport, with black-veiled women wheeling prams and old idlers in faded overalls playing checkers under dusty acacia trees. A telegraph lad is running towards a portly gentleman with a walrus mustache sitting on the edge of the white marble fountain, with the statue of Venus arising out of the sea (modest sea, that)—the gentleman is opening the pink envelope—he bursts into laughter, and reaches in his pocket to hunt for a tip. The dirigible is fifty feet up now—a banyan tree is now concealing the gentleman, but there are five girls in checkered dresses with blue aprons on, waving to some passenger—perhaps a fellow employee at the airport restaurant, headed for a better position in some big city—gone, all gone.

Gaps, gaps, gaps.

The older one gets . . . they're like amoebae, feeding
on some virulent and nutritive broth—they coalesce . . .
the torrent becomes a lake . . . the lake a sea . . . the
sea a blank white . . . like an unexplored area on a map
of Antarctica . . . ah, a few brush marks, like a mus-
tache . . . a hill, a known hill, surrounded by nothingness.

Gaps, gaps, gaps.

Now someone is dabbing tears away, shamefacedly,
while talking about a post-office their grandfather saw
on the Strait of Magellan, with a mountain hanging over
it. Just where the point of rock leaned the farthest out,
a barrel hung by a heavy chain was swaying. A post-
office, with no postmaster, no postman, and no key. Yet—
Ships coming along that way stop and fish out packages
of precious letters that have been dropped into it, to
see if they can find any that want to travel their way.
Sooner or later, a ship comes along, studies the direction
of each package, and says, "Ah, I can take that." Away
she sails, and the barrel swings, doing its duty without
being watched, sending joy to many hearts.

14. *Various Devices*

Might as well lump together info about devices essential to the unfolding of *Moon Canal Morning*—

1. WOLF RING CONTRAPTION

   Inside ring is rubber syphon, leading to a flesh-colored tube along hand and arm (under Gertrud's sleeve)—then up neck and into hair-do. Easy to conceal under a bun. A container (very narrow tube, flattened out like empty toothpaste receptacle) for the simulated blood can be pinned under artificial hair—braids would be very "Gertrud," or hat. Hat optional, but if hat is worn, ought to be something about Gertrud wearing hat in basement to keep hair-do from dampness, or maybe to make Helga feel better about having luncheon in basement—or maybe about her father and double pneumonia—car stalls —heavy snowfall—hospital on mountain peak—dies —G's mother claims because "no hat"—"bad night air" got in car—

2. PILLOW JUICY FART SOUND REGULATOR

   Set off by pressure on chair pillow. Pressure gauge flicks ribbon switch—ten seconds of sound as spool unwinds, then snaps back to starter position.

3. SPIDER DEVICE

Lever releases metal weight attached to wire. Pulls
open stopper of smoke container in light fixture
over participant. Participant reaches innocently for
napkin, plastic tarantula scurries out, up arm, up
onto hair—coincides with smoke effect—thinks
hair's on fire—spider falls to floor—five seconds of
spasms—disintegrates.

Actually, meal never gets eaten in basement. Denoue-
ment of *MOON CANAL MORNING* is this: Gertrud
is just testing Helga, she confesses—breaking point—reveal
buried hostility—passes with flying colors—up to the two
of them to murder Dr. Schmidlapp—dangerous charlatan—
must be stopped—plans are expanding—plus his relationship
with Diana Vienna—

4. MICRO-VOX PELLET

Fastened under hood, connected to screen-o-phone.
Channel B allows caller to reply to answerer,
then flip back to *MOON CANAL MORNING*—
wavy lines are sign it's pre-visualed.

5. PLASTIC FACE

15. *Helga In Java*

Diana Vienna's voice was getting raspy. I asked her if she wanted to take a breather—click. She said not to worry—click. The wavy lines tangled into knots, and then calmed down again. Diana Vienna began coughing . . .

Helga: *I've lost my complete appetite. Luncheon—*

Gertrud: *Sit down. For the last time.*

Helga: *Oh, Gertrud. Before I go to sleep, I make believe you're melted down from my hot breath. I grease myself all over with Gertrud ice and put a little Gertrud slush under my ears so I'll smell nice, and a little Gertrud on my nipples—*

Gertrud: *Sit down. For the last time.*

Helga: *Oh, I hear Gertrud voices singing, coming from my whole body, singing come up the stairs, and I'll pour strawberries all over you, and we'll lick each other clean of red juices, let's not skimp on food, it's a lonely world, don't be so prissy, it's summer, so don't complain about green stains on your behind, we'll be so happy in the grass—*

Gertrud: *SIT DOWN.*

Helga: Of all—Gertrud. Gertrud, this pillow—

Gertrud: Whoop whoop whoop. Hadn't you better go
          powder your—ahem—nose?

Helga: With my body, I'll cover yours.

Gertrud: Now now now. Pick up your napkin so we
          can eat.

Helga: Gertrud, get it away. Get it away! Smoke, my
          hair is on fire. They petrify me, spiders . . .
          Fire, fire . . . how vividly it comes back to me,
          the post-war years. I was on my way to see my
          Dutch-Malay beloved. (COUGH) Hola, the
          spiders in that slum street in Java—I'd taken the
          wrong (COUGH COUGH) turn—in more
          ways than one. I was in a black ante-room,
          resting on an aubergine bench. I ask the Chinese
          custodian in which direction is the Queen
          Victoria Lounge (COUGH COUGH COUGH)
          where a Herr H'wan Boog Ryk (COUGH) is
          awaiting me to take me onto his yacht in the
          harbor, since we are sailing to (COUGH
          COUGH COUGH COUGH COUGH COUGH
          COUGH) Hawaii. One block away, ten minutes
          to kill. Celebrate? Love to. Now we are in his
          basement loving quarters, he calls it. Fizzy
          drink. Woozy . . . I came to in a pagoda
          (COUGH COUGH COUGH COUGH
          COUGH COUGH) with monkeys everywhere
          (COUGH COUGH COUGH COUGH
          COUGH)—one relieves himself, scoops up the
          excrement with a spider imbedded in it still
          wriggling on his finger. He eats it. I throw up.
          The custodian enters. He's in saffron robes. He

*orders me to wear a veil. (COUGH COUGH
COUGH COUGH COUGH COUGH
COUGH) I apportion the grain from the
donations, so much per monk, so much per
relations and hangers-on and various beloveds.
Months pass and pass. Hearing those sutras
helped me find a stoic inner strength that saw
me through the ensuing struggle for (COUGH
COUGH COUGH COUGH COUGH)
freedom, which meant sacrificing human
relationships for the destruction of enemy
machinery, one's single goal in life. In
particular, the steel-blue claw in the harbor that
held us subject. Ah, great sweet bosomy
interludes between bosomy mothers fanning
themselves in the doorways of their hovels and
willowy saboteuses united to free the delicate
young revolutionaries . . . my first assignment.
The Ryk Dye Works. Gutters all around the
plant with loathsome spiders feasting on the
vegetable dyes, their progeny crawling around
the food stalls . . . woozy. Disguised as a
govern—bomb—governess—bomb in pram. A
car pulls up. Police. The needles! Striped straws
everywhere! Liberation! Sucking up the evil-
doers . . . an explosion . . . the steel-blue claw
was no more. In the hospital (COUGH
COUGH COUGH COUGH COUGH COUGH
COUGH COUGH COUGH COUGH
COUGH) the first words I said were—*

Gertrud: *As I've explicated already, we have neither
candles nor music for this luncheon repast. I'm
plain tired. Let's eat.*

Helga: *First, Grace. Say Grace.*

Gertrud: *Grace!*

Helga: *Why must you torture me this way?*

Gertrud: *Whoop whoop whoop. Oh well. Oh God*
(COUGH COUGH COUGH COUGH
COUGH COUGH COUGH COUGH
COUGH COUGH COUGH COUGH
COUGH) in whom we live and move and are,
concede a restoring rain—

16. *Pleasure Vision Labyrinth*

At last. The hooded figure's fingers (left hand) stopped their incessant crablike scrabbling for shelter, and began cautiously edging under Barry's belt—into his pants—only to be rebuffed by a pouncy opponent, judging from their excited retreats back to the safety of the belt. With its right hand, which stopped the figure 8 motion that circled around Barry's breasts, the hooded figure bent the tongue of the belt upwards till it probed Barry's stomach button hollow: 9:46. It was at this point, judging from transitory image reconstructions, that I must have gone into a pleasure vision labyrinth of unusual depth, replete with razzle-dazzle hallucinatory fold-ins of startling rapidity and with a momentary after-effect that was new to me. For a split second, I felt like a Man of Knowledge, safely on my way, rounding the leaf, and in the seat beside me, bent down, probing my stomach button hollow with her tongue, was Diana Vienna, sharing an eternal journey through the stars, just the two of us revolving and revolving, and with time frozen forever at 9:46.

Put my hand in her mouth, trustingly. Using thumb as wedge, pry it open. Her tongue licks my fingers. She looks at me vacantly, as if not too familiar with other human beings—Stone Age eyes. No sense bothering with what such looks mean—it's a different world in which movements are relieved of the weight of cause-and-effect pulley systems which are so elaborate, the effect often has no relation to the cause, at which point good-and-bad judgments are brought into play to tidy up the chaos into a "visible design," and when that fails, a babble of individual voices arises, some clinging to a past that certainly never existed, and some lunging towards a future that keeps vanishing around the corner, down into the subway, up the freight elevator, into the waiting limousine, red light, one reaches into the back seat and grabs a wig-and-veil, the limousine floor has opened, plummeting the pursued one down a man-hole into the sewer system, motorboat, underground river, the ocean . . . no sense bothering with what such looks mean—it's a different world in which seasons change, unobserved and unremembered. We are both back at some kind of beginning, before gravity armaments, big and little, have had a chance to exert their pulls, before the throb of stuff being duplicated at an ever accelerating tempo has brought about a correspondingly dynamic drift towards extinction, with us caught in the middle, in a menaced but homey vacuum, not particularly wanting to annex anything, but not wanting to be caught in a squeeze play either; we must think of the future, and those who will come after us, no? What if they are misshapen troglodytes with puny appendages and running sores with spastic thought processes that deal only fitfully with the problems at hand, waiting the rest of the time for machines to fix things up nice? If their survival becomes more and more precarious, this would be our fault, not that anyone'd be left who'd care. But by annexing too much to gratify our myriad desires, what if we sucked the juices, and left them the hull? On the other hand, by denying ourselves, what if our deliberate slow-down changed from conscious discipline to slovenly habit—the fewer the desires, the fewer the reactions, leading to a sloth-like immobility that seemed "natural"? Upon awakening, no sense bothering with what such looks mean, and the double reflection in those pupils, of someone white-haired and paunchy, and all around—a wasteland of dunes littered with champagne corks, plastic sexual implements, stuffed toy animals—to what end our self-denial? To look into such vacant eyes holds these worriments momentarily at bay, to say the least—and one can enjoy one's three squares a day in peace, passing morsels back and forth, plus deep sleeps, plus love-making, plus eight hours a day, seven days a week devoted to inventing and constructing devices to keep out unwelcome third parties. For a lark, one can stare at one's own image in his/her pupils— nothing consequential—a fun-house perspective, Humpty Dumpty girth, tiny arms and legs that taper off abruptly (a bit too troglodyte for comfort) and elongated forehead —very cucumber, fun-house cucumber, the Cucumber Twins, happy in their cloud land—that is when mist seeps into the cave, our cave. Crackling static: Base Camp. Barry must have news re the Love O' Tomorrow orchid. Ah, he's cracked its code. It's a sentient being intrigued by us two-legged parvenus and our missionary position. Its non-stop observations have an exhausting clarity about them, as rendered by Barry's halting Morse Code rat-tat-

*tat. By paying absolute attention, hands folded in one's
lap, above the sheet, one begins to float along the crest of
a flood. Only the tops are visible—a stony peak here and
there, way above tree level. And as for sea level, the
plethora of busybody tracking stations are blessedly si-
lenced, already half corroded from the waste products
released by huge savage creatures stirred out of the dark re-
gions at the bottom of the ocean by the turmoil far
above. What alternative is there but to listen to the constant
rat-tat-tat—a meandering lullaby about pods snapping open
when the moon is full, releasing seeds borne by wind
currents over barren steppes to distant oases of green, rat-
tat-tat. In those Stone Age eyes, yellow flecks whirl about.
How long have we nestled in each other's arms? Those
flecks have a sadness about them, as tumbleweeds do,
rolling now this way, now that, with an air of earnest
purpose that is not one whit genuine, buffeted by a wind
that just doesn't know its own mind, rolling now this
way, now that, across a prairie that is flowerless, flower-
less.*

17. Cough Cough Cough

"COUGH COUGH COUGH"

Pleasure vision labyrinth over . . . 9:47 . . . "as Gertrud says 'restoring rain,' the washing machine goes kerflooey, and the two women scurry under the table, and huddle in the dry warmth of each other's arms. All kinds of . . .

DINKY THOUGHT CUBE VISION

HUMAN TOUCH

> *for work coll*
> *and employees*
> *for those tan*
> *affected fina*
> *lly inexplica*
> *bly human tou*
> *ch a rumble s*

All kinds of fold-ins . . . Blue Silo . . . FOU . . . supply . . . Savings Bond . . . one's own lifeblood . . . Figure 8 . . . rubber syphon . . . slum street . . . in tepid bath . . . Fat Peak Woman . . . heated mirrors . . . accident

"COUGH COUGH COUGH"

18. *Helga Whispers "Grace"*

> COUGH COUGH COUGH
> "—O God in whom we—"
> COUGH COUGH COUGH

Hooded person unbuttons Barry's fly. Left hand proceeds from one button to next, deftly, with precision, as blue-jeans fall. Hooded person's right hand cups Barry's dick.

> COUGH COUGH COUGH
> "—live and move and—"
> COUGH COUGH COUGH

> > *for work colleagu*
> > *and employees, co*
> > *for those tangent*
> > *affected and fina*
> > *lly inexplicably,*
> > *human touch a rum*
> > *ble seat open wit*
> > *oppet in it cuddl*

> COUGH COUGH COUGH
> "—are we implore thy—"
> COUGH COUGH COUGH

Barry places his hands on hooded figure's shoulders. As hooded figure falls to knees, position angle changes. I see Barry's face. Back of hood bobs from side to side. . . .

> COUGH COUGH COUGH
> "—clemency so that—"
> COUGH COUGH COUGH

COUGH COUGH COUGH
"—thou having made—"
COUGH COUGH COUGH

Hooded figure's head makes T motion, left to right to left, then to middle (along elastic-band of jockstrap Barry wore) then down dick bump (guesswork, can't see

COUGH COUGH COUGH
"to cease the flooding—"
COUGH COUGH COUGH

> *for work colleagu*
> *and employees, co*
> *for those tangent*
> *affected and fina*
> *lly   inexplicably,*
> *human touch a rum*
> *ble seat open wit*
> *oppet in it cuddl*

COUGH COUGH COUGH
"—rain shalt show to—"
COUGH COUGH COUGH

as head blocks it) and back up to elastic-band across to far left. Repeat. Speeds up. Comic metronome—that's what hood looks like! Guesswork, can't see it, sad to say.

COUGH COUGH COUGH
"—us through the calm—"
COUGH COUGH COUGH

COUGH COUGH COUGH
"—sky the hilarity—"
COUGH COUGH COUGH

Hooded figure pulls down Barry's jockstrap; it sticks at his knees. Can't see hardly anything, except hood keeps bobbing back and forth, up and down, very very fast.

COUGH COUGH COUGH
"—of thy face. So—"
COUGH COUGH COUGH

*for work colleagu
and employees, co
for those tangent
affected and fina
lly inexplicably,
human touch a rum
ble seat open wit
oppet in it cuddl*

COUGH COUGH COUGH
"—be it. Amen. Amen."
COUGH COUGH COUGH

Barry's eyes close. Jaws start working, grinding his teeth, must be. Tongue shows between lips, just pink tip. "M." "MM." "MMM." "MMMM." "MMMMM." Yippee!!!!

COUGH COUGH COUGH
"—For all eternity."
COUGH COUGH COUGH

19. *Info Fragments*

1. Barry Wingate lowers head.

2. Ex-hooded person turns sideways. Bobbing continues.

3. Ruddy complexion. Half of face revealed. It's ME! Accident vertigo . . . tendrils . . . steel-blue claw . . . redden . . .

4. Dead-ringer person reaches up to hair, yanks. Left side, then right side. Zippers. Just rubbery stuff with hair attached. Stuffed into pocket. Hair tumbles down, blond. Starts to turn sideways.

5. Barry Wingate waves at me. Politico conquering hero wave.

6. Bobbing person turns . . . tenth of face . . . girl (?) . . . fifth of face . . . fold-ins . . . tepid bath . . . water reddens . . . peeing out . . . supply of one's own lifeblood . . . City Foam . . . half of face . . . autombol . . . FOU . . . moon . . . midget . . . bobbing . . . it's . . . D . . . D . . . Di . . . Dia . . . Dian . . . Diana . . . Diana V . . . Diana Vi . . . Diana Vie . . . Diana Vien . . . Diana Vienn . . . Diana Vienna . . . hein. Hein.

HIATUS: ORCHID ODE

    magnificent knolls
out of which issued forth singing
    mist wisps (love-taps)

    no one on this long long porch
    laughs when I joke about bushes
    the funniness of branches jiggling

    outline at dusk of two breasts
immortals with insomnia arise from the earth at will
    don't remember anything pre-milk

    but that's me agog on the arm akimbo
    no more comfortable then than now
    feigning sleep on the flexed biceps

breather: a violet sky
no—a violent sky with bruises
no—my first purple cloud orchid

soft Southern singing below in steerage
of white protuberances feeding on mere air
on deck a whiff of wet leaves

zooming along groggily
even signposts seemed languorous later that summer
they all wanted to "bum a ride"

hard to achieve a legitimate idyll
hard too to digest seeds on the wing (though birds do)
recent singing (in heavy traffic) keeps receding

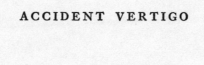
ACCIDENT VERTIGO

Another continent.

Nothing but solitaries around one. One finishes one's coffee, one's lip is bleeding from a metal sliver imbedded in the sugar cube which refuses to dissolve however hard one hacks it with one's spoon, and the spoon handle bends if much pressure is exerted, until it is curved, like an old-fashioned baby spoon. So what is there to do but proceed to the nearest newsstand. All the newspapers have identical headlines:

ACCIDENT VERTIGO!

It's the main topic at parties, or in stalled vehicles in traffic jams, or in cabaret shows in the false city of huts—

> *I dunno where to go,*
> *Got Big "A" Vertigo!*

Time for a relaxing cigarette. The match tip splits, and part of it arcs into a pile of cheap green magazines, the printing machine of which must be on the blink too, as one can dimly see its feature article entitled—is that an "I"—another "I"—is that "GO"—a cinch:

ACCIDENT VERTIGO!

And that smudged part must be—it isn't smudged at all! It's a paper-weight that the vendor's just moved, a joke piece of dog excrement disguised as a cucumber, goes back and forth, back and forth visually—that's the joke—popular gift item in the area, made of two-parts squishy organic food matter, and one-part hallucinogens—so that you not only get proper nourishment, you get proper visual and auditory jolting; it's instructive to follow its progress through the alimentary channels, the beating it takes from various acids, how it gets broken down, courses through the blood system, pellets of it, finally reforming into its original shape, hein hein.

WHOOSH! It catches fire; it's not edible at all. Some paper-weight! Must be made of cheesy plastic, but then the flames are obviously being abetted by the bottle of bootleg wheat mash, ether, and rubbing alcohol the old man is holding out teasingly to the woman selling pencils on the platform with kiddie-car wheels. Where are all the solitaries? Racing down the street, yes, the newsstand's on fire, and the refuse trough beside it—the pencil woman's propelling her platform, the vendor and the bootlegger are struggling to get out of their overcoats—the synthetic fur collars are blazing—but their flailing arms only fan the flames—a tractor's gone berserk—it's hit them —one flattens oneself against a government building—the wall buckles, a family leap in front of one (how lucky they were watching the passing scene from the ornate iron balcony that narrowly misses one as it crashes to the sidewalk) and run off into the night, hobbling, quickly inventing a rabbity way of avoiding the tractors—a veritable armada, some fuel mutation must be speeding them up this way—more coffee? The loudspeakers of the avenue have interrupted a medley of riverboat hosanna songs (needless to say at the wrong tempo, due to a motor disturbance, so they sound like dirges) and are promising free coffee to anyone in the vicinity whose first name contains the syllable "VERT." Most likely this is part of a campaign to change people's responses to such words as "VERTIGO" and "ACCIDENT." A blind woman throws her white cane in the air: VERA, MY NAME IS VERA, GOODNESS HOW LUCKY. She steps into the street—and vanishes! A man-hole: the lids split in two if stepped on if one weighs more than eighty pounds—the sign says so, stenciled on the gutter, though it's true, the "y" has been obscured on the "eight," smudged by time or some vandal. Ah, she's clambering out now, cursing everyone and his Dutch uncle.

Another continent!
Solitaries fretting interminably about damaged candy-bars with dead leaves and wasps in them—the manufac-turer insists these are one-in-a-million lucky prizes, if one plants the leaves, mulching them with ten more crumbled candybars, and then injects the wasps with a side-product (fill hypodermic, special kind, another side-product) called:

VERTIGO!

Another continent!
Rife with rumors, rumors of new regulations! IS THIS HARAPPA? YUSS, IT IS HARAPPA AS YOUR TEECKET STEEPU-LATES. BUT THIS IS MOHENJO-DARO, WITH ITS FAMED RED DOMES, NOT TO MENTION THE MOHENJO-DARO-ESQUE MAN-TRAS BEING ANGRILY SHOUTED BY THE CROWD OUTSIDE THIS

RICKSHAW. YES, IT IS THAT TOO: HARAPPA, MOHENJO-DARO, MOHENJO-DARO, HARAPPA. IT IS A PEERIOD OF TRANSEETION. YUSS?

Nothing to do but sell one's belongings and move to a new commune in the icelands. The solitaries whom one joins, who have the same idea, are already laughing at their having fretted about their candybars named ACCIDENT (printed in yellow streak-of-lightning lettering), piled high in their closets, half-gnawed, with tooth-marks that will actually be a useful record in case they need dental care (icy winds are bad for porous enamel) which is a *fait accompli* (free) according to the new regulations, along with hoes, rakes, shovels, palmetto slats, and valuable vari-colored corn seeds from the vaults of THE MEMORIES, which the commune has been promised access to seven days a week (free), not directly, but via a feeder station that is being hurried to completion, barring certain techni-cal difficulties that have arisen—namely, "gourd notions." Gourd notions? Who knows what that was, before it got garbled by a series of transmission experts. Got no-tions? God nations? Hoarded rations? Border of oceans? YUSS, BORDER CONDEETIONS. The excited voices of the soli-taries, burbling around one! Soon these tubular environ-ments (M they're called, just M)—("*Twelve new M this week, Hashville, Roston, Yrie, Vontpelier*")—("*Why hasn't Texas more M?*")—one watches the cube sliver in one's coffee suspiciously—from the lip pomade that was to have healed the cut, one has caught a skin fungus condition (brown specks that produce spores each summer, giving one's skin a rough sandpaper texture that badly mutilates those attractive bathers one lies next to, then on top of)—ah, safe! No sliver, one swallows the last of the tepid cube with oily Paisley patterns on its surface (good! detergent residue most likely)—

"MY THROAT'S ON FIRE, MY THROAT'S ON FIRE!"—the waitress and counterman dive for the floor, lie there face down as the coffee machine explodes, jetting steam—the specialist says the lip spores are not at fault here. The throat was aggravated by spores from the improperly washed cup, as certain ingredients of the detergent combined with certain ingredients in the cube—the sugar manufacturer obligingly traces them to "unclean" trucks: particles of dust adhered to shipments of alfalfa—it's all immaterial! Time for—another continent. Time for the commune with its guaranteed implements, its solitaries, and access to THE MEMORIES. Yes, soon those tubular environments will dot the land. Tprngfld. Zmpa. Tlata. Thenne. MMs they're now called, jocularly, MMs, by the other solitaries. New regulations. MMMs they're now called, MMMs. Not in personal conversation anymore—speeches mainly. And that's not the only change. New regulations. No implements. No access to the feeder station except for ten minutes every Sunday A.M. at 11—which is just when the inhabitants of the island the feeder station is located on prohibit all communiques to or from the outside world. From 11 A.M. to 12 noon, they sit on the rocks, facing the very continent we are on, and repeat the STONE MANTRAS silently to themselves:

Stone, oh stone of stone, stone of stone stone,
Stone, oh stone of stone, stone of stone stone stone,
Stone, oh stone of stone, stone of stone stone stone stone of stone

All, all immaterial. The regulations have changed again —the commune's area has been assigned to a financieress (the solitaries hiss FINANCIERESS FINANCIERESS so it sounds like THINGS ARE GETTING SERIOUS) who has been given the commune's harvests going back seven years. Harvests! What harvests! Now those tubular environments are muttered about reverently—MMMMMs. Generally in spring, one hears it murmured, someone on the other side of the glacier, one of the original solitaries getting some sun, resting up for the summer: Santa Claus and sleighs and bobbing for pale-green health lozenges jocularly referred to as "ACCIDENTS." The commune is referred to as "VERTIGO." Perhaps some deep-seated need on the part of the solitaries to mention the inevitable and therefore possibly prevent it from ever happening. Debts. Debts piled on debts. Debts! They're as bad as the blizzards that add new and higher levels of snow each year, so that one must continually build additions on top of old roofs to provide sub-standard living quarters, cubbyholes whole units of solitaries are forced to wedge themselves into in shifts—one cuts a door through to the surface—by the time it's finished, it's impossible to open it—the drifts outside press against it. The widow's walk (first year) that came to be regarded as such an oddity (wasted labor) is now a sub-sub-sub-basement, with clumsy drawings pasted on the inside of the windows, scenes of green plateaus, with elks grazing, and throngs gathering for a picnic, with athletic competitions and contests of all sorts (potato sack races, dig-for-the-nougat, the Mine Field)—a fine den to relax in under the gales. The expenses, though. The bally outlay! The financieress proves to be understanding. She knows reinforcements and buttresses come dear these days. Wouldn't it be simpler to start afresh? She cancels the debts. On the spot, she is dubbed mmmmmm. mmmmmm: that's the design decided on for NEW VERTIGO—units of six row houses of double arches, with a snow trough between the arches, snow which will be melted by gas burners instantly at intervals in the trough. New seed arrives—butterbeans from the vaults of THE MEMORIES, butterbeans coded to mutate into oil, gold, molybdenum zinc, tungsten, pre-Bronze Age oxygen—commodities of great value elsewhere—and all because she has constant access by means of a private system of relayed impulses to THE MEMORIES. The nature of that private system she is not at liberty to divulge. But yippee! New lodgements, new eatments, vistas, and a future of green fields that will chomp up the glaciers—with tendrils that will "ossify the snow particles." And then us solitaries can return to the old places and gather around us grateful retinues who'll soften the aging process.

All, all is immaterial. The regulations have changed again. She is not the financieress! She is a politico-socio-economo-opportunist of the rankest order! The genuine financieress arrives, after a saga of mishaps (waylaid, a period in an asylum in a forest, cafeteria work, saves enough to approach a first-rate legal adviser, fights her way through the courts, success!)—and is not pleased by the lay-out, not pleased at all. New debts! New debts piled on the debts! Back to the old buried dwellings that now need new extensions upward with egresses to the surface. Trapdoor egresses at the end of a series of ladders, one on top of the other, each one more rickety than the one before. Egresses that are never used, for the financieress refuses to underwrite the expense of top-grade preservatives for the butterbeans until the butterbeans begin to mutate into the promised valuables. And why else would they be sent to the cities to the north, tubular environments already glutted with mammoth gewgaws. From her lean-to, she smells the rancid night air, and announces to us solitaries:

White fungi are spreading along the new gullies.
Nothing wriggles in the lab with ticketed jellies.

Trinkets—human hair plaited into flower offerings—
thank you for them. I have been in touch with the Mings

and they will set up here a vast pleasure park
of rocks and snow and silence and winds and the dark;

one solitary will be chosen by year, by lot.
Goodbye, all others. Amnesty. No one will be shot.

It is well to be in the flatlands of Texas, my hands spread out on my thighs as I sit, immobile as a quiet and composed Egyptian, posing for a bas-relief of his ruler, head bent down, eyes following the ceaseless bobbing.

Another continent.

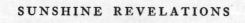

SUNSHINE REVELATIONS

In a situation of such adversity, when the two human beings in the world I felt linked to in a rounding the leaf ecstasy cube way seemed to be maneuvering me into an underground terminus, in which they'd hog the space and use up the air, before vanishing casually upwards, causing a landslide that'd incarcerate me in my new tomb, *c'mon, c'mon*, distant voices shout, *we're not waiting another second*, what else was there to do but stay put, and wait for further developments to unfold around the safety zone of my chair, the chair I'd sleep-walked to, that moon canal morning. Any movement, from instant involvement to sudden departure, seemed brazen under the circumstances—like lustily singing one's national anthem in a leaky dory in enemy waters, when one, sole survivor that one is, has just escaped a burning, sinking luxury liner (*"Around The World Cruise for three, please!"*), only to be rammed by the jagged prow of a fast-moving iceberg, propelled by ocean magnets able to shift and redirect currents and tides. Distant men in distant control

rooms hundreds of feet below the ocean might hear one's
BA TA TA, LA LA LA, OOMPAH OOMPAH TRING . . . (an-
them music) and SAFELY ON MY WAY . . . (anthem words)
—which make wriggly pollywog blips on these distant
men's detection screens, blips that may or may not cause
them to shift nervously in their seats until they con-
tact Dossier City in the far distant motherland, to de-
code the real significance of SAFELY ON MY WAY and BA
TA TA, LA LA LA, OOMPAH OOMPAH TRING—and in those
few micro-seconds that it takes for the machines of Dossier
City to reply BLUE INSTITUTE THORAZINE PIANIST MOJESTA
TWANG IN *way* PLUS GLOTTAL CLICK IN *oompah* TEXAS
HYDROFARMS SUNSHINE TRAFFIC CUBE RESCUE AT ONCE ONE
OF US—the blips fade from vivid aquamarine to washed-
out Blue Baby Blue, leaving ROUNDING THE LEAF (anthem
words) and ZZZZZZZZZZ (anthem music's landlubber—i.e.
"lover"—climax) unrecorded, for the manipulated iceberg
has knifed the dory in two, halving the solitary passenger
rowing with one oar in circles, while paddling with one
half-numb mittenless hand. But who are those folks in
the motorboat, sharing a pair of binoculars, observing the
incident with bemused detachment? There they go, zoom-
ing south to further adventures: The Hooded Couple.

Pleasant but odd to be led by Diana-and-Barry shadows,
looming large on tunnel walls lit by mysterious fires, so
that the beckoning crook of an aquiline forefinger could
be the trunk of a giant elephant upset by strange sur-
roundings, looking for someone to snuff up, poor crazed
hulk. Pleasant but odd this labyrinth of corridors that ap-
pear to be level, but actually, judging from the accelerating
pace of one's steps, is twisting down, far from surface
hubbub, devoid of any periscope through which one can

momentarily glimpse sky chunks, or any leaf, or cloverleaf, or any cloverleaf intersection, or any city, or any Holy City, or any traffic cube, or any funeral cortege with a lucky death midget, or any chihuahua, or any thought cube, or any thought cube exploding with ecstasy releasants, or any orchid, alive and in flower, or any orchid, dead and safely preserved, or any carton, or box, or suitable container of reasonable life permanence, placed under an eye-shaped window in an attic a two-legged sentient being in possession of his faculties could reach via skeletal stairs, stairs that won't give way no matter what their age, stairs safeguarded against and examined for possible sabotage that might topple the ascender into the black abyss below.

One morning, Diana went out by the barn in her hood outfit, and busied herself feeding orchid blooms into the corn machine. Then she kneeled, and her hooded head began bobbing—upside-down T motion. I thought of getting up out of my chair, going to the window, opening it, climbing out, walking across the lawn, tapping her on the shoulder—if only I was wearing a pretzel belt buckle. And pants. Too, at that precise moment, my old familiar Dalmatian dog balls began jockeying back and forth on the trapdoor overhead, lullingly, like slow-motion yo-yos, alternating with an "After you, Alphonse!" politesse, each ball a sensuous Titian breast with mottled pink and black skin, so kissable, lickable, suckable. Devoid of nipples, true, but they smelled of tarragon in a Swiss pantry, with snow falling outside, and youths on snowshoes dotting a glacier a few feet away, climbing up to visit their "psychological wives" encased in clear pale green ice at the summit, smiling in their sleep, forever young.

There she was, face pressed against the window, flattened lips all blubbery and Mayan. Barry too.

Idea for a fantastic psycho-surround! According to a highly confidential survey Barry slipped under my door, private traffic on the National Traffic Cube (NYC–LA, LA–NYC) "will soon be permitted five hours a week;" program repeats cause accidents ("time woof distortion")—drivers confuse previous trip with present one, act irrationally, disrupting the rounding the leaf tempos to such an extent the coverts become overloaded, causing jam-ups, with disoriented individuals wandering about on foot, even jumping off the ads, expecting to ascend into the clouds (mangled corpses)—much to the chagrin of the Environment Comptrollers. Hence, there's a crying need for five-hour psycho-surrounds.

THEME: Individual survival via diluting of instinctual reactions. Replace them with artificial colorations that fit any situation.

EXAMPLE: Hussar faces screaming tribesmen (mob rule) converging on his forest outpost tower with its transparent polyethylene floor. He glares down through the floor at the spear tips. Loses monocle. Gropes his way along floor on all fours, peering. Tribesmen squint at his chest tattoo: GIRLIE IN UNDIES IN PHONEBOOTH GOING OVER NIAGARA FALLS—"LONG DISTANCE, PLIZZ!" Tribesmen bow down. Not worship. Just grateful for a light moment which leavens the soggy tempo of jungle warfare. They leave him alone to resume his meditations about country house weekends in the nineteenth century, when Diana Vienna (in white dress made of bloody bandages—Crimean War) sauntered down a leafy lane (cholera epidemic) twirling her parasol (venereal disease) with netting (addicted to laudanum) over her face to protect it from the sun (unwanted pregnancy), making it hard for her to hear the badinage of her escorts, dapper toffs (urine-soaked bread) discoursing on the wild berries (specialty houses) they've gorged on in the hinterlands (chimneysweeps).

Note Left Under The Welcome Mat: I appreciate the time and trouble you're both taking. Not a day goes by that I don't think of you both. Lying there in the hammock —it was like being thrown against an electric fence, hurtled into nothingness. A bug bit me. I let it—I couldn't hit it. What one represses one second emerges two seconds later hideously distorted (dog ball into timebomb), and four seconds later crops up, an archeological find: another round-faced death deity to stick up on the shelf and forget about. Lying there in the hammock, naked, in the middle, a reversal took place. Diana, I confess I've always been afraid you'd vanish into the sky above at any moment. And there I was, positioned in a sky above your sky, floating freely, looking down at unused Diana penthouses camouflaged as water towers to keep out unwelcome visitors, and unused Diana hideaway gorges, cliff dwellings empty. In city after city below, Diana ex-intimates were peering up, waiting for the sky vehicle to descend, and you to alight. Lying there in the hammock, naked, in the middle, I wondered if living in the sky, in perpetual transit, won't frazzle your nerves. At which point my trick-knee bonked you in the jaw, Barry, just as your tongue began probing wet ringlets in my armpits, the better to tug at them with your teeth, happy *frisson*, just as Diana's prehensile toes were yanking out my first white pubic hair. A merry linking up process, what with the rainbows flowing upward out of the grass and into us—

the jungle in a good mood, wanting to tag along with—
Gloop-silv.
Gloop-silv.
Best to you both from here on in,
                        Love,
                            Gloop-silv

Please fetch me the match-wrapper. It's in the forest,
a little ways below the tree line, where the big black
boulders take over. They inform me testily: there's no
mountain hereabouts. There was one a while back, but it
was chopped up into hydrofarm sluices. Wanna see the
sluices, they chortle. Just Texas flatness, we thought you
knew. Above us are stars try as you may you can't see
'em budge, they chorus. A sop, but a sop that doesn't
dispel a stupid longing for up-and-down vistas, and the
rough-and-tumble of hot gushers wetting icy slopes. Lap,
lap, lap go the lagoons on Christmas Day, and with all these
legs interlocked, and the sun going down, a sunburn, and
the flamingo feathers and all—a tepid tub, lots of red-
nesses, red eyes, red lips, red privates—

Diana wants a light. Then why did she blow out the
match? Or was it the air purifier vent, as she claims,
the one that sounds like a happy person humming when
the three of us fall silent. Or was it that she objected
to me trying to read my own handwriting, holding up a
new list of experimental sequences to try. Not necessary,
such lists, but that's why they're fun—leading to spats,
anecdotes, confessions, touchy moments, kinks, "the end,"
"the beginning," whole hours that become interestingly
flowing because *déjà vue* spreads from one person to the
next to the next, we're all in it, entranced, literally, whose
stomach is rumbling, mine, no, yours, the red parts get

all mixed up, what belongs to who, until it stops, jolting everyone back into a plainer scene, slower and less open to possibilities, a scene where one watches one's step, out of habit, without letting the others know one is doing so.

The sequences are opening up, of their own accord. A "contemporary feel" is taking over—time and energy aren't wasted on you-do-this-and-I'll-do-that conventions. No, the sequences flow into each other, innocently—unconcerned with those grandiose forms that create replicas, panoramas, naturally, of full rich lives lived to the fullest.

Anecdote about Mrs. Tyler. The day before my arrival in Texas, in order to perfect their "joke" on me, Barry and Diana had to solve several mechanical difficulties, re the screen-o-phone system and *MOON CANAL MORNING*. Poor Mrs. Tyler kept answering the kitchen screen-o-phone (circuit foul-up) only to hear *O GOD IN WHOM WE LIVE AND MOVE WE IMPLORE THY CLEMENCY* (pre-visualed by Diana)—at which point Barry's voice'd cut in with an exasperated *HERE THE MACHINE STOPS* (spool snarls, bollixing up this test section). Mrs. Tyler, a devout believer in Galactic God and Devil Rays (and in an imminent apocalypse if the devout didn't keep a sharp look-out) succumbed to nervous prostration. *HERE THE MACHINE STOPS* sounded to her like the end of the world, especially as, each time she answered, the screen-o-phone voice had slid up or down a notch in what sounded ominously like jungle animal Devil Ray blasphemies—the result of Barry's fiddling with the micro-vox pellet adjustors. Gorilla yawp: too low. Parrakeet twittering: too high. Yawps and twitterings that set her parrot off into squawked repetitions of *HERE THE MACHINE STOPS—HERE THE MACHINE STOPS—HERE THE MACHINE STOPS.*

Mrs. Tyler was beside herself, what with the buzzes, the weavy lines going every whichway, and the various voices controlled by demonic Galactic Rays, spewing out unconscionable blasphemies. Horrendous, horrendous: Devil Rays in the upper stratosphere were beaming acids into the mind-cells of mosquitoes, who, by biting jungle animals, altered their chromosomes, hurtling them down the path of evolutionary development till their minds could fixate on blasphemies, and the gift of gab (yawp, yawp, twitter, twitter) was theirs, beamed into screen-o-phones the world over. And what if these mosquitoes bit the watersnakes who slither through the sluices of hydrofarms in the area? What if these watersnakes urinated in water that, several stages later, might end up on our night tables? Trace elements of Devil Ray acids would infiltrate into our mind-cells: blasphemies, whoosh, end of world! At which point Barry unsnarled the spool, and got the screen-o-phone in the guest bedroom to work properly. Diana's voice resumed its normal timbre: *SO THAT THOU HAVING MADE TO CEASE THE FLOODING RAIN SHALT SHOW TO US THROUGH THE CALM SKY THE HILARITY* and so on and so forth. The poor dear was in a euphoric state—the world was saved, Diana'd been chosen a Galactic God Ray Receptor, ah the hugs and kisses, followed by a feast: yam pie, snow-on-mango pudding, and, at Diana's request—bouncing bunnies. All during the feast, her parrot kept squawking, much to their amusement—*HERE THE MACHINE STOPS—HERE THE MACHINE STOPS—HERE THE MACHINE STOPS.*

Working away at my round Barry-and-Diana flag: three silhouettes lying in a hammock, outlined against a blood-red full moon. The hammock interstices are hard, not to mention getting dimples, nose crinkles, and puckered lips right—especially as someone outside my room is distracting me by striking a match, again and again. I can almost hear the little flame go out. Our room, I should say. Sweaty panties are draped on my still unopened "Holy City" valise that Barry refuses to divulge the combination of, not that I care: who has the time! On the safety zone chair arm is a towel with maroon dried-crust spots, gray places where the fibres are matted, an eyelash imprint staring up, various hairs. On the Explorer Pyramid— a black sleepmask. Next to it, crumpled on the floor: The Hood. Propped up in a corner, a homemade psycho-surround, blinking and chattering away—us, some night not long ago: some recent pleasantness.

Cough cough cough. Someone is inhaling. That would be Diana, if we weren't starting to cough alike, laugh alike, moon alike, moan alike, pant alike, "MMMMMM" alike. Smoke is wafting through the keyhole. Time to pee: intermission.

What's this? Someone's unraveled the silhouettes. In their stead, an apoplectic face: Dr. Schmidlapp.

A wind starts up. No, it's the air purifier vent, working overtime. No, it's the whoosh of a huge erection pushing its way through the Barry trapdoor into the Diana non-attic above, luckily empty, so nothing valuable'll get smashed or squashed. How tactful of them not to notice, to go on chatting of moving into a "lighthouse" together, just the two of them. There they go, climbing up its side without further ado. Some stunt, must take years of training, or else they have special shoes. Now they're at the top, FEEL ANYTHING, they shout down. Feels like a caterpillar walking on one's lips, looking for a scrap of leaf, the idiot. This is too complicated to shout, so I just yodel, SURE, SURE. WHA? they yodel back, SHOWER?

SHOWER? as they start to investigate the opening at the top, descending head-first; only their shoes are visible in the mirror suspended above them—a hot gushy flood is pushing up, the fools, watch out, out it pours, YIPPEE! —they'll drown—so far up they can't hear, thanks to this new chorus of "MMMMMMs." WHA? WHA? Looks like it's my turn at the top of the lighthouse, only the air's going out of it; theoretically I should be able to see for miles, if only unexpected descents didn't make my ears pop, but it's exciting, hanging on for dear life, time to put it away in moth-balls, till the next season starts—time to open my eyes, to find they are lying on each side of me, reaching across to touch each other, without touching me. Their warm presences are a blessing.

There's been a request, no, two—for "air." Translation: whoosh, whoosh—the windy season's just begun.

Dr. Schmidlapp was on the screen-o-phone! He looked wan in the afternoon light, bundled up in his deck-chair on his cabin cruiser in the Gulf, Gertrud and Helga on either side of him. We climbed back into bed, me in the middle as usual, and relaxed as the reminiscences of a born raconteur poured out.

"... *opera company stranded in Sofia* ... *fund-raising performance a desperate expedient to effect an immediate departure* ... *happily the theatre was packed* ... *extra hired for a few* ... *cigarette girl in the Brown Derby Scene screamed out* STEEL-BLUE CLAWS, STEEL-BLUE CLAWS *in the middle of Gertrud's big aria* ... *hurled her prop cigars at some invisible assailant, cigars that hit outraged dignitaries in the front rows* ... *curtain was rung down, the crazed girl fainted at Gertrud's feet* ... *brouhaha broke out in the lobby* ... DEMAND OUR MONEY BACK ... *company remon-*

strated with the management . . . resume the performance
. . . out of the question . . . DEMAND OUR MONEY
BACK . . . aging Brunhilde broke down the door of
Gertrud's dressing room as Gertrud fled down the fire-
escape, carrying the crazed girl home to her basement
room in the palace of a local patron of the arts . . . yes,
Helga was her name . . . in that same palace at midnight
that very night . . . in the packed ballroom I began a
lecture on Personality Envelope Builder Uppers in a Feudal
Society . . . practicality of coats of arms when hysterical
screeches . . . STEEL-BLUE CLAWS, STEEL-BLUE
CLAWS . . . outraged dignitaries rushed out . . . poor
creature . . . huddled under a table by a laundry tub
. . . hurling invisible cigars at some invisible assailant . . .
Gertrud sang away . . . ladies and gents . . . do not
interrupt our rehearsal . . . what is more vulnerable,
Baron, than a work of art in its incipient . . . THE
GUTTER IS THAT WAY he hissed . . . I stepped
forward . . . Mesdames, I would be honored to . . ."

One big Boom Town around here, these days. Gushers
a-plenty, share and share alike, no lode is off limits, no
cache sacrosanct. Plenty more where that came from,
where we've come to. These days, weeks—every day's
Mardi Gras, except we skip the masks and parades of
interminable floats to get to the climax: us. These days,
weeks, months, it's hard to remember what life was like
in the old country, where the norm was plod plod plod,
365 days a year, with just the one day off (time off for
good behavior)—a holiday in a Tunnel of Love, in a
papier-mâché grotto (no pets, no visitors), to provide gig-
gling couples with a head above water to ogle, a solitary
silhouette, as they bump bump bump along in their out-
rigger canoes, leis rustling. No time in this Boom Town

(pop. 3) to gear one's emotions towards some modest reward in the future: grotto for three, easy on the phosphorescent glow. Developing and diversifying new desires while keeping track of the old standbys is a fulltime job that takes the nerve of an impresario, the cunning of a venture capitalist. If this peak activity, inner and outer, could be shown on graphs (no time)—the black lines would keep bursting up, up, up—out of their rectangles! There's no way to show qualitative improvements—they have to be taken on faith. In simple physical terms, areas of the body no one would bother about in a month of Sundays are now points of interest, considerable interest, hallowed to fanatic and non-fanatic alike. Backwaters of the mind where tizzies, middle initials, wobbly likes and dislikes might remain unremarked and unremembered are now of paramount concern, mythic import. Eureka, this B-D-Me sufficiency of abundance will make tall tales come true at a dizzy pace full of madcap zest. Eureka, B-D-Me dirigibles will fill the sky with pretty money and magic magnets to tug jewels out of the earth. Our sky. Our earth.

What about the folks we've left behind, Diana wants to know, cough cough cough. Hadn't we better enclose our Boom Town Picnic in a social lab setting, cough cough cough, so glum throngs can press against one-way observation windows to scrutinize our sequences to their heart's content, with re-runs in slow motion, if need be, to catch the nuances. Life styles in the old countries might alter, so one could walk out onto their highways and byways and feel the energy flowing out joyously, into one, full of happy abandon. Barry chimes in—low-energy lives—sucky structures—the individual fixated as embryo in the sac of the—leaks—whereas high-energy lives with closed circuits no longer need to imbue governing bodies with their wishes, umbilical ties, and nightmare screams. My

reaction: what if the glum throngs are made up of King
Kongs who want a lick, a tweak, a freaky cluck, a lucky
fluke, a sticky suck, a beauty fuck, they'll run amok:
STEEL-BLUE   CLAWS,   STEEL-BLUE   CLAWS.
Goombye, observation windows, Boom Town, goombye,
population zero.

Dr. Schmidlapp was back on the screen-o-phone! He
looked shrunken in the purple dusk, at his desk, Gertrud
seated on one side, Helga on the other. We climbed back
into bed, me in the middle, as usual, and relaxed as the
reminiscences of a born raconteur poured out.
   "... *in Baden-Baden* ... *a certain Miss Delight Hag-
gerty manifested an intense interest in furthering my re-
searches* ... *a quest for a safe and sane personality en-
velope builder upper releasant* ... *my final goal, an elite
of hand-picked geniuses working at top capacity, guar-
anteeing universal peace and brotherhood* ... *lowered her
lashes demurely* ... *Miss Delight informed us that her
station in life was that of governess* ... *a firm disci-
plinarian of the old school* ... *couldn't reveal the iden-
tity of her charge* ... *of Scotch-Irish extraction, she
was somewhat schoolmarmish* ... *time was, to her, a
series of semesters* ... *every aspect of reality needs must
be graded on a scale that ranged from A+ to E—* ...
scenery, weather, erotic adventures ... *saw herself pro-
ceeding through life's tests with a respectable B average,
neither too brilliant nor too* ... *'Nae wonder mae success
ae roulette last nicht wae less 'an spictaculair-r-r, dear-r-r
Smythelapp, f'a' ae mathematician, ae best ae deser-r-r-ve
ae B Grade, nae?'* ... *'Ortolans in coffins ae a' vur-r-r-r-y
wae, dear-r-r-r-r Smythelapp, bu' ae'll hae ae bubble-
and-squeak, f' a' ae scaler-r-r-r-r ae gastaenomical heights,
ae deser-r-r-rve ae B Grade, nae?'* ... *late one night,*

Gertrud, seeking to join Helga and myself in our living death meditations, blundered into the wrong mud room, only to discover our Miss Delight hurling muck gobbets at a swart figure wearing only a white, rather soiled, satin sash cluttered with glittering medals, a personage Gertrud recognized at once as the El Presidente, with life tenure, of a misbegotten mango archipelago . . . with a forced smile, she purred, 'Ah, so you're the charge of Delight B Grade.'" . . .

It's as if the green fields all around Barry-and-Diana-and-me have been sucked up into a vacuum cleaner, in the interest of national hygiene. No more side-by-side-by side flattened areas to incite love-starved fat locals. No more footprints heading now this way, now that, with the party in the middle being carted along upside-down, judging by the telltale indentations made by the index finger—an H, an E, and L—another L, upside down, with the extension growing fainter, didn't have time for the O, unless, as a joke, P—in any case, just the four footprints marching neatly along at this point—yet, how messy: picnic detritus, webs of spittle and sperm wobbling on the weeds that flourish in the shadow of the blinking NO TRESPASSING sign ten blocks long and twice as tall. Perhaps some latterday de Medici will provide an artificial field surface, a lush lawn of green needles that can pierce steel boots, like the kind outside Northwest Territory forts in old-time documentaries, the kind that bring Mounties and Eskimos and the last of the sourdough trappers together in an amicable compound where they take turns playing shuffleboard under sunshine simulators, right out in the open, wearing nothing but BVDs handpainted with work-up-a-sweat-and-the-lustier-they-get hula-hula chomp-chomp 'gators, and all around them, to keep them

on the straight and narrow, the Perma-Sizz-Lawn, so hot
dumb bugs flying over it just curl up and drop, soot
specks soon blown away by special vents designed for
just such a purpose, blown away back into the blizzard
that surrounds the compound, not that the menfolk pay
it any mind, scratchin' their balls right out in the open,
beer bellies hangin' out, waitin' their turn, as usual.

As usual, we started with her little toe (left foot), rac-
ing each other just for the heck of it, working over each
toe till she gave us a satiation signal (three quick tongue
clicks): Move Along, Lads. As for the gaps in-between—
some nips and up-and-down-and-around-we-go licks, ta-
pering off with a tickle culled from a Tibetan manual:
"slowly flutter eyelashes like dying hummingbird wing"
—sometimes, accidentally on purpose, my lashes tangled
with Barry's: perfect teamwork! All the while, tip pressed
against tip, our dongs confronted each other, enclosed in
the moist hot tunnel of her store-bought Giantess Hand,
a pulsating apparatus with black talons, wens with clumps
of coarse hair, and a rippling expanse of lubricated skin,
soft as a baby's eyelid, firmly attached to her wrist by
leather straps.

Round about her right ankle, I felt my tongue touch
Barry's eyeball, which jerked back and forth in blind
delight as I heard the three clicks: Move Along, Lads. I
felt myself freeze into total immobility. Before hurtling
myself into the inevitable loop-the-loop saturnalia up
ahead, I felt compelled to wait for a "real" signal, a
genuine go-ahead I'd recognize intuitively the moment
I heard it. What would this "real" signal be? Surely not
this thought cube vision of a banner, projecting itself on
her ankle, a banner with an apoplectic face on it prac-
tically snapping at me, blocking my way, and, all the

while, in the other lane, the open one, a parade of tired but happy revelers streaming past me, down the hairpin curve, coming from the Gala. The Gala where I'm expected momentarily. If only I didn't have to wait for my pesky signal! Pesky banner. What about *my* lane? It's *its* turn. The Gala'll be over. *Is* over.

No one to talk to but an old deaf butler, mopping up the mess, downing unfinished drinks, pinkie extended, as he belches. Nowhere to go but upstairs, where all along the circular corridor, from behind every locked door, orgasm sigh after orgasm sigh issues forth. Hour after hour. Some Gala! No sense choosing a door to pound on, to smash to smithereens—that way, one'll never hear the long-awaited "real" signal, especially as such signals are rare birds these days, being part and parcel of an earlier time, the time of the Founders, whose most ordinary utterances carried for vast distances across the wilderness, golden arias enchanting homesteader and nomad alike. That being the case, no sense waiting around for some one-chance-in-a-million signal, a fluke, to get one back on the track—not with so much high-energy jamming going on around one: orgasm sigh after orgasm sigh, hour after hour. Some Gala. Just dreams, most likely, a rather cheesy cause-and-effect set-up: the sleeping guests are pushovers for still more wish-fulfillment, hence the sighs. Hour after hour. Some dreams! The juicy kind one hears about but never gets a good look at on a frontal, 20–20 vision basis. A buttock vanishing around a kiosk as a plain-clothesman arrests you for "not wearing a thick black face-and-body veil": that's as close as you generally come. A seductive wink that turns out to be merely a nervous tic —peered up at from a vantage point underwater, as you struggle against the undertow to gain time to make doubly sure—that's as close as you generally come. Hour after hour. If a dream that takes a second can seem to last a lifetime, then these sleepers, lucky devils, must be rocketing through whole centuries, cocooned in ecstasy. Only why are the transoms freshly bricked up, and why nary a scratch? Orgasm sighs, pfui! Must be some old blue movie, one print per room, with the same segment, the climax, repeated and repeated. Or a newfangled pleasure contraption blaring away; it works by "suggestion," so the sleepers won't dream the same dream everyone dreams from the cradle to the grave: YOU ARE BIRD FLY INTO SKY BYE-BYE. Measly fodder for wish-fulfillment, admittedly—flying around through the blue, with no particular identity, just an overwhelming sense of loss. But one shouldn't expect flashy myths and grand operas and extravaganzas to spiral out of psyches exhausted from waiting for a "real" signal to get them back on the track, exhausted from boning up on newfangled protocol on how best to obtain newfangled requisition forms for newfangled pleasure contraptions tailored to the newfangled individual "guaranteed to intensify sensory feedback"; "guaranteed to catapult you into archetypal magnetic fields where instincts, long dormant, will erupt with cataclysmic force"; ". . . all the genuine go-aheads you've always . . ."; ". . . handle input at the genius . . ."; ". . . won't ever dull out on you . . ."; ". . . orgasm sighs, hour after hour . . ."

"Requisition forms have taken off as a 'form'—a runaway express chug-chugging pleasure-principle-pleasure-principle-pleasure-principle every mile of the way," explains the loudspeaker, in time to the snapping of the banner with the apoplectic face on it, blocking my way. "Instead of questions to be answered in depth, while tired but happy revelers stream past you, and pesky waivers to be agreed to in triplicate, and passed back and forth for

a mutual OK that needs outside verification, you'll have
delightful drawing room badinage to help you sail through
your retirement program—just mark X in the chortle
circles as you go, and fill in the guffaw squares, and
don't be alarmed if regulations dot the page—they'll en-
hance your over-all enjoyment, wait and see if they don't.
Regulation: badinage must be played against the thud
sounds of an advancing army of irregulars. Regulation:
yellow dust must filter down, stirred up by the mistral
whining just outside the French windows. The subject,
you, can barely hear himself/herself at the white piano,
singing "Gazebo Deb," a ditty about a debutante in a
gazebo who croons an insult song within earshot of her
fey beau. Revealing the depths of his feelings, must croon
how he's the gloom in her curfew, orchid attic, not the
spume in her surf, you are bleak as a week on a mountain
peak, eye-shaped window, all alone with a bone and a
stone telephone, coming to grief rounding the leaf—"

Our first simultaneous three-way orgasm sigh! The two
of them hugged and hugged me, proud giants, almost
squeezing the living daylights out of me, crouched over
that right ankle, still waiting for that signal.

Dr. Schmidlapp was back on the screen-o-phone! In
his private sauna, he looked like a pawn—a helpless
baby mahatma squashed between two regal figures. We
climbed back into bed, me in the middle as usual, and
relaxed as the reminiscences of a born raconteur poured
out.

"... accepted Miss Delight's most generous invita-
tion ... perfect haven for my personality envelope
builder upper research ... Gertrud and Helga intrigued
by the challenge of our new life ... established our-
selves on Miss Delight's luxuriously appointed mango finca,
a gift from the El Presidente, whose red-roofed palace

*loomed above us, a scab on the breast-like volcano that,
according to the islanders, disgorged black clouds of
welcome perfume that could keep one forever young and
beautiful, if swallowed, red-hot . . . happy-go-lucky na-
ture . . . always laughing . . . soon made the fascinating
discovery they had no concept of death . . . patois has
no verb TO BE . . . closest equivalent is MAKE HA-HA
SOUND SURF—i.e., MAKE JOKE . . . TO DIE is
TO PLAY SLOTH FOREVER . . . OLD MAN MAKE
HA-HA SOUND SURF PLAYING SLOTH FOR-
EVER = OLD MAN IS DEAD . . . PLAYING SLOTH
FOREVER was considered a sign the person desired to
be eaten by his beloved one or ones . . . supplanted by a
tradition now prevalent . . . shrinking and embalming
. . . kept around the PERFUME GLAND (house) . . .
chat with them . . . carry them into the eating pit . . .
place food before them . . . fall in love with them . . .
woo them and wed them . . . often crowded out of house
and home by hundreds of these ancestor mummies . . .
HA-HA SOUND SURF early in life . . . BABY MAKE
HA-HA SOUND SURF (is) DEFECATING ON THE
SLEEPING SUNBATHER . . . to Helga's astonishment,
the child's mother smothered the child with . . . POST-
MAN MAKE HA-HA SOUND SURF (is) DELIVER-
ING AN IMPORTANT LETTER . . . 'Dear Dr.
Schmidlapp, Your application for research funds has been
OCEAN SUCK and we anxiously await a detailed
MANGO FLIRT . . . by midnight, December 31st . . .
before LONELY MAW . . .'—key words had been scis-
sored out, and two-word classic poems had been inserted:*

> *OCEAN SUCK*
>
> *MANGO FLIRT*
>
> *LONELY MAW*

. . . December 31st deadline had long since passed, and a false return address had been pasted on . . . awoke in the night laughing . . . happier than I'd ever been . . . illumination . . . here was the personality envelope builder upper right under my nose . . . HA-HA SOUND SURF . . . MAKE JOKE . . . that very night I began my first experiment . . . STRIPED STRAWS MAKE HA-HA SOUND SURF SCRATCHING AT HELGA'S WINDOW AT MIDNIGHT . . . Helga ran screaming into Miss Delight's room . . . threw herself into her arms . . . vulnerable state . . . panic . . . Miss Delight comforted her . . . 'ae A-plus, gir-r-r-lie . . . A-plus' . . . confessed her secret longings ever since Baden-Baden . . . both came down to breakfast at noon . . . roses in their cheeks . . . Helga announced she was moving into Miss Delight's room . . . 'A-plus, nae' . . . second experiment . . . Gertrud manipulated the striped straws in the moonlight . . . crashed through the window . . . hovered over them, entwined in bed . . . Miss Delight screamed . . . Helga's choked gasp . . . I concentrated hard . . . 'HA-HA SOUND SURF' . . . 'HA-HA SOUND SURF' . . . forced my thought-waves into Helga's brain . . . heard a snicker . . . a titter . . . another titter . . . a hoot . . . a cascade of rich, unadulterated Grade-A-plus laughter . . . gave the signal to withdraw the straws . . . happy discovery . . . incredible finding . . . years of fear erased . . . positive results . . . myself into further experiments . . . great satisfaction to see Helga and Miss Delight strolling hand-in-hand through the orchid garden . . . radiance . . . Gertrud grew silent and morose . . . meals in her room . . . touched a morsel . . . listlessly flipped through the pages of opera scores, humming snippets from death arias . . . decided to undertake a further experiment using myself . . . darkened room . . . sound of her

breathing heavily . . . brushed her exposed nipple with stuffed tarantula . . . screams . . . DR. SCHMIDLAPP MAKES HA-HA SOUND SURF (is) SEDUCING GERTRUD . . . transformed by my own experiment . . . in love . . . eagerness to try again . . . DR. SCHMIDLAPP MAKES HA-HA SOUND SURF (is) PROPOSING MARRIAGE . . . tarantula costume . . . tickle her with hairy appendages . . . roared . . . accepted me in between gales of . . . transformed . . . lost all interest in further experiments . . . in idyllic surroundings, the four of us . . . picnics on the mimosa cliffs . . . volcano lip glows at sunset . . . one afternoon, a cloud of magenta butterflies . . . feeding on our arms . . . the El Presidente summoned me to the palace and delivered an ultimatum . . . household informants had kept him apprised of the love-fest at the finca . . . Miss Delight's lethargy during their weekly discipline session was ruinous to his morale . . . reins of government were slipping from his . . . crime against the state, so to speak . . . his one dream . . . make Miss Delight his First Lady . . . 'nae' . . . unable to use force . . . obvious solution . . . up to me to marry Helga . . . bound to so hurt and shock her . . . rebound . . . accept him of her own free will . . . political intransigeance . . . outrigger canoe with meagre supplies . . . 'fishing expedition was lost' . . . returned down the funicular to the finca with a heavy heart . . . no one I dared to confide in . . . state of profound dejection . . . situation hopeless . . . concentrated hard . . . HA-HA SOUND SURF . . . HA-HA SOUND SURF . . . the personality envelope builder upper supreme . . . Miss Delight left for her tryst with the El Presidente . . . suitcase laden with disciplinary equipment . . . tearfully promised Helga it was the last time . . . Gertrud and I exchanged toasts as we watched the volcano turn orange at sunset, swinging in the hammock on the verandah . . . 'to us' . . . 'counting the days' . . . refilled her cocoanut cup . . . 'losh of litter ones' . . . 'ush' . . . lifted her onto the chaise 'lounge' as she pronounced it . . . sprinkled the rest of the smelly root flakes on a bed of heliotrope . . . girded myself . . . HA-HA SOUND SURF . . . HA-HA SOUND SURF . . . sneaked up behind Helga in the orchid garden . . . nape with stuffed tarantula . . . firmly on her breast . . . DR. SCHMIDLAPP MAKES HA-HA SOUND SURF (is) SEDUCING HELGA . . . night of unbelievable happiness . . . once again transformed by my own . . . no limits to this personality envelope builder upper . . . silhouetted by the sunrise . . . orange beams slanted across the bed . . . licked the crust of sleep sand from her eyelash and arose . . . climbed into the costume . . . hairy appendages . . . roared . . . accepted my proposal . . . gales of . . . transformed again . . . Gertrud . . . bloodshot eyes glaring through her tangled hair . . . CHEAP WHORE'S TRICK . . . HEARD EVERY WORD . . . LAST MAN . . . DRINK . . . GUTTER WHERE I FOUND YOU . . . framed by the window, Miss Delight, freshly picked bouquet in hand . . . shrieks . . . spat out the bitter petals . . . buried my head . . . slammed doors . . . silence . . . that afternoon a jubilant message from the El Presidente arrived . . . consented to be his First Lady . . . send for her personal effects . . . ceremony that very evening . . . double wedding feast at the finca . . . 'hereby . . . mango finca . . . wedding present to you and Helga . . . research funds . . . honor to the archipelago!' . . . dusk . . . official arrived . . . undressed us . . . lay down on the grass . . . handed us a mango . . . shared it . . . three of us . . . embrace . . . three of us . . . shower of petals . . . 'man and woman' . . . become . . . 'man-woman' . . . Gertrud stared at us from the hammock on the verandah . . . cold eyes . . . time for the midnight feast . . . cabinet ministers and their wives . . . diplomats . . . stuffy atmosphere prevailed . . . at last the El Presidente . . . carried a large bird-cage . . . draped with the national flag . . . FAVOR-ITE PET . . . EXHAUSTED FROM THE WEDDING, THE FIRST LADY SENDS HER REGRETS . . . Helga dutifully sat in one bridal seat of honor, next to the bird-cage . . . Gertrud nowhere to be seen . . . proceed without her . . . petty functionaries anxious to display a Euro-pean façade of culture and refinement long since van-ished back in . . . slatternly islander in bedroom slippers . . . reeking of cocoanut wine . . . tureen of yam soup splashed over Helga's wedding blouse . . . lace clung to her flesh . . . revealed red bite marks and purple bruises . . . shocked clucks . . . I fired the harridan at once . . . silent feast . . . stared down at their plates . . . the El Presidente lifted the flag to feed his silent pet tidbits . . . to the salon . . . Helga and I arm-in-arm . . . facing us in an armchair, skirt hiked up, turban askew, feet propped up on the liqueur tray, smoking a stogie . . . CARE FOR A PUFF, STEEL-CLAW? . . . pelted Helga . . . me . . . the diplomats and the Cabinet . . . contents of the box . . . GENTLEMEN, MEET MY RESEARCH ASSO-CIATE . . . HA-HA SOUND SURF EXPERIMENT . . . the sound of exploding cigars reverberated from the foyer, the driveway, the very sky as the funicular, with its party of dignitaries . . . noticed the El Presidente sobbing, kneeling at her feet . . . BE MY FIRST LADY . . . DEAR SIR, YOU ALREADY HAVE ONE . . . lifted the flag . . . the cage was empty but for a fragment of singed scarf draped across the little swing . . . recogniz-able plaid . . . sprawled among the sunflower seeds, a doll, a perfect replica of Miss Delight . . . LEAPT INTO

THE VOLCANO . . . AFTERNOON DRIVE . . . BE-
SEECH YOU . . . handed Gertrud a fresh box . . .
START . . . a firm no . . . found ourselves at dawn . . .
glow of the volcano lip at dawn . . . outrigger canoe bal-
ing furiously . . . white yacht . . . screamed our lungs out
. . . launch . . . the three of us were soon reclining on
deck-chairs . . . Mr. Ott . . . an automobile magnate . . .
I CAN CHANGE YOUR LIFE, MR. OTT . . . PER-
SONALITY ENVELOPE BUILDER UPPER . . . our
life together had begun . . ."

Mrs. Tyler's favorite word is "discombobulated." If
there's bird-seed in the scrambled eggs, it's because she
got "discombobulated" thinking about a trip she took
through the ghost towns of the Old West, where spit 'n
whittle geezers rocking on the front porch of the last
remaining rooming house mutter shouting-at-a-deef-gov't
speeches:
White Anger . . . Kicked The Old Sombrero . . . Dis-
combobulated . . .

"What a nice thousand-mile-long roller-coaster ride that
was, with handsome Ute braves offering us pipes through
the windows in the quaint depots, and Ute girlies fed
us sweetmeats manually, and wove us flower jewelry out
of strands of our hairs and wigs, jewelry that fanned
out into Elizabethan ruffles so big we couldn't get our
heads in, and before we knew it, there we were, chugging
through the Rockies, staring at each other when we went
around curves in the canyons, all those coaches with all
those faces . . . put on our best smile and wave to beat
the band . . . talk about discombobulated . . ."

Sinking back into the familiar . . . beach resort ocean

. . . summer . . . squiggly red blobs . . . not sea-water
. . . it's beef jelly and the red blobs have already developed
spines that are uncurling, knobs that are forming fangs,
fangs in jaws that go clack clack clack. Who's the scientist
in control around here?

Dr. Schmidlapp was on the screen-o-phone! He was
wearing pink face powder, and his hair was urine-blond.
He was sleeping as he whizzed along in the limousine,
past the hydrofarms, with Gertrud and Helga on either
side. We climbed into bed, me in the middle as usual, and
relaxed.
" . . . appreciate your co-operation, Barry, and you too,
dear Diana . . . power surging through you thanks to
your personality envelope builder upper par excellence . . .
ha-ha sound surf . . . liberate Zoroaster . . . psycho-files
. . . carry on my experiments . . . the three of you . . .
time to look out the window . . . binoculars . . ."
Helga reached into her handbag, and extracted a pair of
pliers. She bent down out of range of the screen-o-phone.
" . . . tie on the old feedbag . . ."
Dr. Schmidlapp's voice was silenced. The screen-o-
phone faded as Helga's lips began to move, repeating the
same movements.
Steel-blue claws? Steel-blue claws?
Barry fetched the binoculars. On the highway cube, a
freight-train chugged along, past vast factory roofs with
great brand-names slanted towards the sun. Not five hun-
dred yards away, in the lane nearest us, a procession of
vehicles moved slowly along, their headlights on—the fu-
neral of a notable, judging from the number of vehicles
involved—three omnibuses, many station wagons, a large
bunch of sedans and coupes, and, bringing up the rear,
the traditional finishing touch: a roadster with a good-luck

moppet in the rumble-seat, chihuahua staring sideways.
No dirigible. No monoplanes. No circle of postmen on
stilts. No mail-sack dropping. No man in tux rising out
of the flowers. No man passing out brief-case.

Idea for a fantastic psycho-surround!

THEME: The metal branches clink against each other.
Central plaza chimes bong away unattended. No one
knows how to do it manually, thus everyone must go a
separate way—down a path to a wooden gate at the foot
of a hill, all divided up into a series of squares one can
pass through at variable speed. Through the branches,
the sun can be glimpsed.

EXAMPLE: We will sleep some more, as the juices in our
bodies settle against each other.

Another fantastic psycho-surround!

THEME: Fragments of partially decodable papyrus mys-
teries curl, brown, and burst into flame without any
warning, because of some magnifying glass in the distance,
angled by a hitchhiker in a truck speeding along the
traffic cube.

EXAMPLE: The sun goes down, while chimes bong and
bong away, and helplessly, in an empty, final square, we
head our separate ways.

Following Barry's explicit instructions, I took the valise
propped against the chair, and placed it on my lap, lock
side up. Two pointers were attached to a dial. One pointer
was large and black, the other small and green. White lines
fanned out from the dial, on which two concentric circles

were marked. The black pointer was for the white lines fanning out on the larger circle. The green pointer was for the white lines fanning out on the smaller circle. The smaller circle was made up of the following capital letters and punctuation marks:

ADJMOS—()

The larger circle was made up of the following uncapitalized letters:

acdefhilnoprstuy

I twirled the green pointer to "J." Then the large black pointer to "a," around to "n." Then the green pointer again: the "dash." Back to the "M." Then over to the black pointer—from "n" back to the "a," then all the way around to "r," then a good ways back to "c," then around to "h." Then over to the green pointer: the first parenthesis—"(," then back to the black pointer, which was at "h." Back to the "f," around to "i," around to "r," a slight twist to "s," another slight twist to "t," then back to "l," back to "e," back to "a," and around to "f." Back to the green pointer: the other parenthesis—")." Back to the "A." Then, using the black pointer, from the "f" to the "p," a slight twist to "r," then over to the green pointer, the "dash," then back to the "J," then over to the black pointer. From "r" to "u," then back to the "n." Then the green pointer. "(." Then back to the black pointer, from "n" to "s," way back to "e," back to "c," forward to "o," back to "n," then back again to "d," forward to "l," back to "e," back to "a," and around to "f." Over to the green pointer: ")." Back to the "J," then over to the black pointer, from "f" to "u," quite a sweep, and back to the "l," then another big sweep over to the "y." Over to the green pointer for the "dash," then back to the "S." Then over to the black pointer for the "e," going the long way around, from "y," then over to the "p," then a short jaunt to the "t." Then over to the green pointer for the "(," back to the black pointer, "t," second one in a row, then the "h," a slight move to the "i," over to the "r," back to the "d," then the "l," back to the "e," back to the "a," then forward, at last, to the "f." Then over to the green pointer for the ")." Using the green pointer again, back to the "O," then over to the black pointer. A slight backward twist to the "c" from the "f," then over to the "t." Back to the green pointer. Back from the "O" to the "D," then over to the black pointer again—all the way from "t" to "e," then further back to "c." Then the green pointer again: "(." Then the black pointer. From the "c" to the "f." Then over to the "o," and over to "u"—

I burst out laughing. I'd left out the "dash" between the "t" and the "D."

A throbbing filled the air. I peered out the window of my bedroom. A Blue Silo Hydroplane approached directly overhead. Its shadow almost blotted out the traffic cube rising just beyond the serrated roof of the Wingate Barn.

Two blue ropes were let down, with hooks at regular intervals on their interior sides. The shrill throbbing of the motors above was deafening, and a fierce wind beat against the side of the barn, exposing the silvery undersides of the leaves of a grove of espaliered peach trees.

A blue sack dropped down out of a square opening between the hydroplane's landing discs, wavering from side to side, landing on the lawn gently. A second sack positioned in front of the tunnel beneath Barry's sleeping quarters was hooked onto the blue ropes by Barry and

Mrs. Tyler. The blue ropes receded into the sky, carrying the sack with them. Bye-bye.

Barry motioned to me: the new sack was for me: my orchid box.

With no Diana, it's hard to buckle down to the five-hour psycho-surround for the NYC–LA, LA–NYC National Traffic Cube. Barry doesn't see much point in my thought cubes, but—

un-patches warm
led arm-hair sl
t it painfully!
ver that the tr
m is working in
harmony with it

rolled up the heat fr
m the sun-patches war
ming their frizzled a
rm-hair slightly isn'
t it painfully obviou
s to any discerning o
bserver that the traf
fic system is working

in total harmony with
itself, that each, ye
s, intersection provi
des each participatin
g individual with a s
ense of being exhilar
ated as the effortles
s starting and stoppi
ng unfolds a successi
on of variations, alt

LETTER-POEM TO A HYDROFARM

Dear B-and-D, we are all thriving here: routine established.
Gertrud and Helga spent the day on the lagoon, snoozed
      and fished.

I mastered the combination on the valise, which blessedly
      unlocked.
My "Holy City Geography Book" looked so drab I was
      shocked.

The authors' names had faded. No Bishop T. L-W Dao.
      All I could see
Of Rev. Annie Muldane was ANN and the final E.

No Fr. Sculler. All that was left of Rabbi Borg was OR.
I opened to the end-paper. No sky, no traffic cube, no
      car.

Just a black nose and two paws. Chihuahua! The CHI
      part.
And a small "d" inked into the cloth (gave me a start)

By you, Diana, that day you became my prophecy
      collator. I closed the book,

Went to my attic-bedroom-den, and, on my mouth
     organ, played some Gluck.

Under the eye-shaped window, I contemplated the Orchid
     Box.
Beside it, on a table made of orange lava rocks

Lies The Explorers' Pyramid. Next summer, I intend to
     visit Nirgu—
tooth tattoos, sad mules, rope bridges—poisoned stakes,
     boo!

Dumb to travel when I'm really putting down roots.
The N. P. Region (including Liana and Harry) is filled
     with deaf-mutes

But they don't bother us, and we don't bother them.
The Research Plantation is, for all its "being over" air,
     a gem.

On cool nights, we picnic in a hammock attached to
     Calvin's Shrine.
Surrounded by orchid bushes, his marble ruffle shimmers
     in the moonshine.

The local Environment Comptroller pays us an occasional
     call.
We get drunk on cocoanut wine. He reels off, "Sisal
     festoons . . . wall."

Soon we'll start the project: to construct a human-sized
     orchid plant
with interchangeable private parts. Don't say we can't—

We can! With erotic psycho-surrounds (get 'em while
     they're young)
the future of mank—drat! If only the air didn't smell of
     dung.

Hard to get started. But have no fear. Repeat, have no
    fear.
ANN plus E plus OR plus CHI plus d—good omen.
    ORCHID YEAR